ESSENT...

PORTUGAL

TRAVEL GUIDE

Plan, Visit, Discover Hidden Gems, and Experience the Art, Culture, History & Splendors of Portugal

Craig Langbourn

Table of Contents

Introduction

When I got off the aircraft, I took in a long breath of the warm, salty air. I could immediately feel the thrill swelling within me - I was finally in Portugal. I had always dreamt of seeing this magnificent nation, with its quaint towns, gorgeous villages, and spectacular scenery. And now, here I was, eager to explore it all.

I recall the first time I heard about Portugal. My grandpa, a seasoned traveler, had recently returned from a vacation there and was talking about the picturesque places, the great cuisine, and the kind people. When he showed me photographs of the colorful streets of Lisbon, the famous port wine cellars of Porto, and the magnificent beaches of the Algarve, I knew that one day I would have to experience it all for myself.

Years later, when I finally got the chance to organize a vacation to Portugal, I was beyond delighted. I spent months researching places, reading travel books, and chatting with people who had been there. I wanted to make the most of my vacation and explore as much of the nation as possible.

I made my way to the railway station and started my trip to Lisbon, the dynamic capital of Portugal, the city that would be my home base for the next few days. When I took in the sights and sounds of the city, I couldn't help but experience a feeling of astonishment. I spent my first few days exploring the historic neighborhoods of Alfama and Baixa, admiring the colorful buildings and the unique tilework known as azulejos, the narrow cobblestone streets, trying the local cuisine, and taking in the stunning views from the city's many lookout points, and the lively atmosphere all combined to create a truly magical experience. I also indulged in the exquisite seafood and pastel de nata, the famed Portuguese custard pie.

I also took a day excursion to Porto, the second-largest city in Portugal and the origin of port wine. I was impressed by the grandeur of the Douro River and the antique port wine cellars that bordered its banks. I spent my days roaming through the Ribeira neighborhood, enjoying the beautiful buildings and drinking the local wine. At night, I was amazed by the vibrant nightlife scene of pubs and clubs. Undoubtedly the city had a great combination of history, culture, and heritage

Yet the highlight of my vacation was probably the Algarve. The southern coast of Portugal is heaven for beach lovers. I spent my days lazing on the gorgeous beaches and exploring the rough coastline. I also took a boat journey to the Ria Formosa Nature Park, where I saw flamingos and other unusual species.

When my journey concluded, I couldn't help but experience a feeling of loss. I had fallen in love with Portugal, and I knew that I would come to return one day. But for now, I was pleased to carry with me the memories of the lovely locations I had been to, the amazing cuisine I had eaten, and the wonderful people I had met. Portugal had captivated my heart and I knew it would always retain a special place in it.

Welcome to the country of sun, sea, and history – Portugal, with its attractive towns, lovely villages, and magnificent scenery, this nation has something to offer any tourist. From the busy streets of Lisbon to the quiet beaches of the Algarve, and from the lovely wine region of Porto to the natural beauty of the Azores, Portugal is a location that will leave you fascinated and wanting more. So, pack your bags and join us as we uncover the mysteries of Portugal.

In this travel guide, I will take you on a tour of the most beautiful and intriguing destinations in Portugal. You will find the greatest things to see and do, where to eat and drink, and where to stay. I will also give practical advice on organizing your trip, including visa and passport requirements, health and safety, currency and budgeting, and cultural norms and etiquette.

When you click through the pages of this book, you will get a flavor of the rich culture, history, and people of this great nation. We hope that this guide will encourage you to plan your next trip to Portugal and explore the hidden beauties of this lovely nation for yourself.

We'll introduce you to the culture, traditions, and people that make Portugal so distinctive and offer you all the practical information you need to organize your trip. From the ideal time to visit the must-see sights, to the greatest places to dine and drink, this guide has got you covered. So pack your luggage, grab your camera, and join us as we unearth the mysteries of Portugal.

Chapter 1

Explore and Experience Portugal

Portugal is a beautiful and culturally rich nation with lots to offer travelers. From its magnificent beaches to its dynamic cities and quaint villages, Portugal is the ideal place for a diverse and enjoyable visit. In Portugal, there is something for everyone, from the exciting nightlife of Lisbon to the breathtaking architecture of Porto and its neighboring towns, as well as the pristine beauty of the Portuguese countryside.

Exploring Portugal is a terrific opportunity to discover the distinct culture and breathtaking beauty of this lovely nation. Situated in the southwestern region of Europe, Portugal is recognized for its magnificent beaches, bustling towns, and vibrant culture. Whether you're a newbie tourist or a seasoned adventurer, Portugal has something to offer everyone.

While visiting Portugal, you may discover its various attractions, including its dynamic cities, beautiful towns, and magnificent beaches. Lisbon is one of the most popular cities to visit, with its cobblestoned streets and breathtaking vistas of the Tagus River, gorgeous architecture, active nightlife, and world-renowned food, Lisbon is the ideal destination to start your Portuguese experience. Make sure to explore some of the city's notable sights, including the Jeronimos Monastery, Belem Tower, and the Sao Jorge Castle.

Porto, the country's second biggest city, is recognized for its bustling nightlife and its picturesque old town. Other popular cities are Coimbra, Faro, and Braga.

While visiting Portugal, it is also worth seeing its rural regions. There are numerous villages and small towns dotted over the nation, each with its particular character and charms. For example, the Douro Valley is famed for its wines and magnificent landscape, while the Algarve is a popular destination for its stunning beaches and vibrant resorts.

Lastly, Portugal is also home to some of the most stunning and untouched landscapes in Europe. From the Douro Valley to the Serra da Estrela mountains, Portugal is rich with spectacular outdoor attractions and is the ideal trip for nature enthusiasts. Walk or cycle across the gorgeous landscape, or go horseback riding. For the most daring, there are lots of water activities such as windsurfing, kiteboarding, and kayaking.

No matter what style of trip you are searching for, Portugal has plenty to offer. Whether you are searching for a busy city getaway or a calm country hideaway, Portugal offers it all. Make sure to visit some of the local markets, where you may get fresh fruit, seafood, and traditional delicacies.

Top Destinations

Exploring Portugal is a terrific way to get to know this lovely nation. Portugal is a tiny nation in western Europe renowned for its magnificent beaches, pleasant weather, huge personality, and diversified geography, culture, and food. Portugal has lots of fantastic spots to

visit. Whether you're searching for a calm beach trip or an action-filled adventure, Portugal offers something for everyone.
These are some of the greatest sites to visit in Portugal:

Lisbon: Lisbon is the capital of Portugal and a must-see destination for every visitor. The city is loaded with colorful streets, great architecture, and lots of cultural events to enjoy. From the famed Jeronimos Monastery to the medieval Alfama area, there is enough to see in Lisbon. Make sure to visit the Belem Tower for beautiful views of the city and the Tagus River. Explore the various museums, monuments, and sights in the city, or take a day excursion to one of the local beaches or villages.

Porto: Porto is Portugal's second-largest city and a renowned destination for travelers. The city is recognized for its gorgeous architecture, cobblestone streets, and wonderful gastronomy. Spend some time touring the ancient city center, seeing the many churches and the famed Livraria Lello bookstore. Don't forget to try the local Port wine while you're in town, or take a boat trip down the Douro River.

Algarve: The Algarve is Portugal's southernmost area and heaven for beach lovers. With its magnificent coastline and crystal-clear oceans, attractive villages, and abundance of outdoor activities.
It's little surprise the Algarve is one of the best tourist destinations in Portugal. Spend some time exploring the region's beautiful beaches and take a boat ride to explore the coastline and observe some of the region's magnificent animals.

Azores: The Azores is an archipelago in the Atlantic Ocean and a favorite destination for nature enthusiasts. The nine islands of the Azores are home to beautiful scenery, including lush forests, volcanic lakes, and jagged coasts. Spend some time exploring the islands and take a boat excursion to view some of the region's wonderful wildlife.

The Douro Valley: This magnificent area of Portugal is famed for its wines, undulating hills, and ancient towns. Enjoy a tour of the vineyards and try some of Portugal's famed wines.

Sintra: Sintra is a famous location for visitors and residents alike. The city is recognized for its gorgeous palaces and gardens, as well as its closeness to Lisbon. Spend a day touring the Moorish Castle and the Pena Palace, both of which are UNESCO World Heritage sites. Make sure to take the time to explore the various cobblestone streets and charming cafés in the city center.

Advantages of Traveling

Seeing other locations and cultures, even only for a few days, has been demonstrated to actually 'make a difference to our mental health and enhance our lives in ways others can't. These are simply six methods how:

1. It makes you happier- The most apparent reason for traveling is because you wish to and it makes you feel good. The prospect of escaping run, 9—5 work, or loud neighbors for a short time is undoubtedly enough to bring a grin to your face. Additionally, research from

Cornell University reveals that when someone spends money on an experience, they have a longer-lasting feeling of enjoyment than if they were to spend money on a tangible thing (Eilers; 2020). Hence, it is reasonable to claim that having a flawless holiday experience would boost your life satisfaction

2. It permits you to detach and recharge your batteries. Taking a break is vital for everyone. After you enter adulthood, you spend a lot of time working or caring for others, which might make you feel quite exhausted. Holidays are the ideal excuse to abandon those chores for a bit and take some time to refill your energy levels. You'll then be able to return home feeling rejuvenated and even perform better. If you don't take this time away, you may end yourself suffering from burnout, stress, or even anxiety.
3. It makes you healthier: if you spend a lot of time inside for work or reside in an area that doesn't receive much sunlight, traveling on vacation to someplace

brighter may enhance your health. This is because our bodies require vitamin D to be able to operate efficiently, and our bodies only naturally make it when exposed to the sun. Thus, if you fail to safely acquire the required amount of exposure for your skin tone, you might be short on this crucial vitamin and in need of a little top-up; the ideal reason to sunbathe! Depending on where you travel, you may also find it easier to acquire fresh fruit, fish, and vegetables, and be able to walk more than you do at home, which will both enhance your health and fitness.

4. You'll be exposed to things: it is fair to claim that if you opt to go on vacation to someplace you've never been before, it might offer you a fresh and fascinating view of life. Even merely taking a trip along a different route, hearing new languages, or opening your draperies to seeing a fresh perspective Will be life—enriching and a terrific way to develop beautiful memories. You'll be exposed to new cuisine, customs, people, and

places which you will be able to look back on with love.

5. It increases social, communication, and language skills: If you travel someplace where the local language is different from yours, getting engaged in learning at least part of it may perform wonders for your brain by enhancing its memory function Throughout time. While overseas, you'll get to meet and talk to individuals from diverse walks of life and participate in conversions you may not have done at home, making you more compassionate and giving you a larger perspective of the world.
6. It helps you appreciate nature more: while picking a location to visit, a lot of us like to look for nations or regions that give us access to nature, whether it be beaches, woods, or simply, sunlight. This may help us genuinely appreciate Mother Nature's beauty and in turn, be more willing to care for the earth for future generations.

Of course, there are so many more perks and reasons to travel, and having visited the globe for 15 years myself, I can tell that will never get enough of it. I have been to locations and plan to visit so many more in the future since I liked the experience, particularly my time in Europe. When I visited Europe for the first time, though, I made a few practical blunders which meant that I lost out on building a lot of great memories.

I recall traveling to Italy with two full luggage and a carry-on. As we arrived, the weather was brilliant and I was thrilled to explore, but after getting off the airport and reaching the gorgeous city of Florence, I had to haul all of this stuff along the cobblestone paths; it was awkward and a practical nightmare! I also didn't have an action for my stay, so chose to simply "wing it," which sadly meant that I didn't get to do all the activities I now know would have been accessible to me. When I traveled back to Italy, I had a well-planned schedule and considerably less baggage, and I'm delighted to Announce that I had a vacation of a lifetime. My original less-than-perfect travel experience is why I am writing this book; I want you to learn from my prior errors and enjoy your holiday to the utmost.

Another destination I liked visiting was Portugal and I am so pleased that you are making plans to travel there too! It is a jewel in Europe and can't wait for you to take up everything it has to offer. It has seven unique regions rich in cultures, history, great food, and sophisticated wines, not to mention the popular beaches and various scenery, so let us discover this fascinating nation together.

Why visit Portugal

Portugal is a pleasant and sunny southern European nation on the Iberian Peninsula. It borders Spain and is situated on the Atlantic Ocean, thus it has numerous lovely beaches and a great culture of seafood; salt cod and grilled sardines are the national delicacies. Even within its about 55 –thousand-mile area, it provides a diversified ecosystem which makes it an intriguing and gratifying location to visit. For instance, the Portuguese Azores are rugged and volcanic; the Alentejo is calm and traditional; while the Algarve, a famous tourist region is full of beaches and greenery (Shercliffy 2019)

It's generally warm temperature and 3000 hours of sunlight each year make it a wonderful vacation location all year round. You will need to select your area intelligently depending on your liking since the weather changes substantially from one region to the next (Portugal Climate Information, 2021). For example, certain sections of central Portugal experience colder winters than the rest of the nation even enough snowfall in the mountains to ski. The summers in southern Portugal tend to be quite hot and dry with a nice wind. however, in locations like Madeira, the winters are mild and the summers are more pleasant with subtropical qualities. Lisbon, the capital city is famed for its sunny weather; colorful architecture, and friendly residents. and amazing nightlife, so whatever your age or hobbies you are guaranteed to discover an area that draws you.

If you wish to experience all of these various landscapes and climates by visiting numerous places. No problem! you be able to travel to this varied nation quite simply and pleasantly by automobile. since no two attractions are more than a half-day drive from one another and going to the road is regarded as safe for visitors. By driving yourself around. you •will also have the advantage of being able to see little-known places and little towns that major excursions don't generally go to.

Discovering the Charm of Portugal

One of the greatest ways to appreciate the beauty of Portugal is to tour its capital city, Lisbon. Here, travelers may experience some of the country's most renowned sights, such as the Belem Tower and the Jeronimos Monastery. The city is also home to some of the top restaurants and pubs in the nation, so be sure to taste some of the local specialties.

The nation is also home to some of the most gorgeous beaches in Europe. Portugal offers over 1600 miles of coastline, and the beaches here are recognized for their golden sands and crystal-clear seas. The Algarve area is extremely popular since it contains some of the nicest beaches in the nation.

When it comes to visiting the countryside, Portugal has lots to offer. From the vineyards of the Douro Valley to the mountain peaks of the Serra da Estrela, there is something for everyone. Nature enthusiasts will be impressed by the gorgeous environment, while history aficionados will enjoy the numerous historical monuments dotted over the nation.

Portugal is also recognized for its lively cultural and music scene. The Fado, a classic Portuguese music form, has been designated by UNESCO as an intangible cultural treasure. Tourists may also enjoy classic Portuguese events such as the Festas de Junho in Lisbon, or the Festival of Sao Joao in Porto.

Lastly, no vacation to Portugal is complete without experiencing the native food. Portugal's gastronomy is known for its use of fresh, locally sourced ingredients, and the nation is home to some of the greatest seafood in the world. Don't forget to taste some of the renowned Portuguese desserts such as pastel de nata or the custard tart.

From the picturesque towns and breathtaking landscapes to the lively culture and great cuisine, there is plenty to explore in Portugal.

Whether you are a nature lover, a history buff, or a gourmet, Portugal is sure to fascinate you with its beauty and culture.

The History

Portugal's past is incredibly rich and full of mythology, myths, and conflicts with proof of it still lingering in many locations. It has ties to Iberian tribes, Celtic people, the Roman Empire, Germanic Kingdoms, and Muslim invaders. Portugal also underwent the Christian Reconquista, which occurred when Christian nations tried to regain land from the Muslim moors.

In the first century B.C-E., Celtic tribes invaded the Iberian Peninsula and established the so-called Iberian tribes, producing what is today known as the Celtiberians. The Lusitanians, who occupied the interior area of Portugal from the Iron Age, then fought the Romans for decades until the death of their king, Viriathus who is recognized as a Portuguese hero. The Romans had a considerable effect on the building of the nation and left baths, temples, bridges, and sculptures that may still be seen across the country today. In reality, the name Portugal has a Roman influence since it stems from Portus Cale, which is a hamlet near what is now- the city of Porto.

For many centuries following this, and until an independent kingdom was created, the descendants of the Romans and the Lusitani lived under Moorish rule: those from North Africa. Portugal then moved on to perpetual war and competition with Spain and finally became Europe's Greatest and wealthiest empire. Regrettably, most of the empire was eventually lost, although Portugal held considerable influence over its African coast, Southern and Eastern Asia, and South America, therefore the language being spoken in some of these regions of the globe today. Fast-forward to the mid-1970s when there was a nonviolent revolution that turned the nation from a dictatorship to a democratic republic. Thus, as you can see, Portugal is one of the oldest nations in Europe and claim that understanding its history is to comprehend the streets, appreciate the gorgeous monuments on every corner, and know the psyche of the Portuguese people.

The Beautiful People

More than nine-tenths of the Portuguese people are ethnically Portuguese, but there are also minor numbers of Brazilians, Han Chinese, Africans, and Asians, all of who prefer to have Portuguese as their first Language; nevertheless, many typically also speak English pretty well (Shercliff, 2019). The Portuguese are recognized for being pleasant; easy-going, and highly family-orientated, which is possibly why the atmosphere always seems warm and family-friendly, with plenty to do for a variety of ages. Family is vital in Portugal, therefore don't be shocked to find the intergeneration Sunday lunch custom being up kept to this day.

You will probably be made to feel completely at home as long as you respect the environment and culture. Many Portuguese individuals will go out of their way to assist you if you become lost, for example. They are recognized for being incredibly proud of their nation and culture and view our trips or even moving to Portugal as an honor.

Food and fine coffee are also highly important to Portuguese people, and they love to show it off! Meals are typically fresh and healthful with fresh fish and meats being a mainstay of the local cuisine. Coffee tends to be popular, not necessarily because of the quality, but because of the chance it affords to have a discussion and catch up on life with passers-by. Diet differs throughout the nation, but no matter where you travel, I'm confident you will love many delicacies that delight your taste senses!

There will also be no escape from soccer when you visit Portugal since it is the favorite national sport among residents. They are enthusiastic and even emotional about the sport and when the national team plays, the whole country will gather behind and support them. Everyone is incredibly proud of their soccer players, and with good reason, since Portugal has born some outstanding players such as Eusébio, Luis Figo, and the world-famous Cristiano Ronaldo.

Customs and Practices

Every nation has quirky and distinctive features that make it memorable, and Portugal is no exception; therefore knowing them in advance will them appear less weird to you and you'll be less likely to go against any of them and attract stares. For example, Portuguese people prefer to welcome everyone with a kiss, or two or three, and not only the first time they someone, but every day, so you could witness this charming greeting occurring around you. As a stranger, it is unlikely you be expected to take part, but if the need takes you, at least you know how to blend in. some people also think it disrespectful to eat on the street since meal-times are regarded as holy, special events, and should be savored at a table. If you are a non-smoker who doesn't like being around the smell, or smoke of tobacco, you should also note that the Portuguese are still permitted to smoke inside, but most places will indicate if they tolerate it or not, so you can avoid these areas as possible; a blue sign in the window for "allowed" and red sign for "not allowed."

Other traditional practices incorporate festivals, cuisine, and religion. Santos Populares, which translates into "popular saint's festivals," is the most frequently attended event in Portugal, taking place throughout June across multiple days and nights. Each Portuguese area has its saint, honoring them at various periods of the year, but the most vibrant in June, since it has numerous street celebrations and official holidays. Everyone comes in the streets 'Which are decked ' With colorful balloons and garlands, the fragrance of street food is in the air, and there is a distinct and dynamic atmosphere, making it one of the greatest times of year to come if you truly want to observe authentic Portuguese traditions and culture.

You should also attempt to witness the celebrations in Porto around this time, as they have a specific customer in that the locals will carry small plastic hammers in their hands and beat their pals on their heads with them, all in fun, of course. Around midnight there is then a stunning fireworks show over the Douro River, and people make a wish as they release hot air balloons into the night sky—a lovely sight!

Usually, people would then remain up till the following day to see the sunrise on the beach

Dining with the is another ritual that has weathered the test of time in Portugal, and this is known as Domingos em famíiia which translates as "Sundays with family." From grandpa to baby nieces and nephews, everyone is welcome to indulge in traditional Portuguese dishes, such as the delicious francesinha. 'Which is a ham and cheese toasted sandwich; the filling Carne de Porco á alentejana which is a mixture of diced and fried clams, pork, and potatoes; or the fresh codfish cake, bolinhos de bacalhau, and so much more.
As Portugal is still quite a religious country, many of its popular traditions are steeped in Christianity with locals and visitors taking part in pilgrimages to Santuåvia de Fátima if they feel as though they are going through a difficult time. The most popular time for this is May, as it is believed that in May 1917, three shepherd children saw the Blessed Virgin Mary. So if you visit during this time of the year, it is likely that you will see people walking on the side of the roads, traveling long distances to pray at the holy shrine of Fatima.

Broader Geographical Covering

Portugal shares the Iberian Peninsula with Spain, but it is only roughly one-sixth as big as its neighbor. Combining the Azores (Açores in Portuguese) and Madeira, the nation has a total size of 92,080 square kilometers. Portugal is on the westernmost point of continental Europe. The rocky Pyrenees Mountains divide Iberia from the center of the European continent, while Portugal is even more off over the immensity of Spain. Distance and isolation have developed in Portugal a notion that it is a part of Europe physically but distinct from it culturally, socially, economically, politically, and even mentally. Even in the early 1990s, Lisbon (Lisboa in Portuguese) was a two-to-three-day journey from Paris.

Portugal is surrounded on the west and south by the Atlantic Ocean and on the north and east by Spain. The country's form is that of a rectangle, with its short sides on the north and south and its long sides on the east and west. Portugal's Atlantic coastline is 837 kilometers long; its northern and eastern boundaries with Spain are 336 and 839 kilometers long, respectively.

Historically, Portugal developed as a distinct nation amid centuries of war with the Spanish regions of León and Castile. Even hundreds of years after breaking free from Spain for the final time in 1640, anxieties lingered in Portugal that it may one day be swept up by bigger and more powerful Spain, possibly not militarily, but culturally and economically. Such an idea is conveyed by the Portuguese saying that "neither a nice breeze nor a good marriage ever came from Spain." However, Portugal's long coast has given it an "Atlantic vocation" and drove its past enterprises of global discovery and colonialism.

Portugal is not a homogenous nation geographically. The physical environment varies greatly, generating various diverse geographic zones that, in turn, have affected the culture of the people and their economy and society. Northern Portugal is a hilly, wet area, distinguished by numerous small farms and vineyards. The Portuguese nation formed in this area, battling against León and Castile while concurrently forcing the Moors south and finally off of the peninsula. It is a bleak region of rocky slopes where smallholders have eked out a modest livelihood for hundreds of years. This area is also regarded to be the birthplace of the strongest Portuguese national values of hard labor, thrift, traditionalism, Roman Catholicism, and pragmatism. It is also a region, though, that has lost many of its residents via emigration.

Central Portugal, between the Río Douro in the north and the Rio Tejo (Tagus River in English), encompassing the capital city of Lisbon and its surrounds, is less homogenous. The central coastal region consists of dunes and pine trees, and many inhabitants of the area make their income from fishing. The middle eastern parts, known as the Beira, consist of largely small and medium-sized farms, with some mining and minor industries. The greater Lisbon region, encompassing both the city and its suburbs, accounts for much of the nation's trade and most of its industry.

Southern Portugal, known as the Alentejo is a region of gently sloping hills and plains characterized by enormous estates with large-scale agricultural and livestock. It was formerly also a place of frequently disgruntled tenant farmers and peasants. In contrast to the conservative north, the Alentejo was an area of radical political activities; for a long period, the Portuguese Communist Party (Partido Comunista Português—PCP) was the dominant party in the province.

The farthest south of Portugal is known as the Algarve. It is an arid area of smallholdings, grazing, fishing, and coastal communities. This is the part of Portugal most heavily impacted by the Moors; even now the Moorish influence is visible in the region's speech and architecture. With its mild temperature and Mediterranean sky, the Algarve has also become a hub for tourism and home to many international retirees.

Traditionally, Portugal was organized administratively into six provinces that matched closely to these natural geographic boundaries. The north consisted of two provinces, the coastal Minho and the inland Trás-os-Montes. Although, the center was made up of Beira and Estremadura provinces, while the south consisted of the Alentejo and the Algarve. Subsequently, these historical provinces were further partitioned for administrative reasons, but the historical designations have been kept in common use.

Even though it is a tiny nation, Portugal offers a vast diversity of landforms, climatic conditions, and soils. The biggest distinction is between the hilly areas of the north and, across the Río Tejo, the huge rolling plains of the south. Within these two primary areas are smaller subcategories that represent the country's significant disparities. The Minho and Trás-os-Montes are both hilly, but whilst the former is green with copious rainfall, the latter is arid and parched. The Beira Litoral and Estremadura are younger geologically and comprise sandstone, limestone, and volcanic rock. Beira Alta (Upper Beira) is hilly and creates a barrier across the heart of Portugal, whereas Beira Baixa (Lower Beira) is arid and windy, an extension of the Spanish plains. The Alentejo comprises moderate hills and plains. Since it is one of the driest locations in the nation, it is not appropriate for intensive agriculture. The region does support cattle ranching, as well as cork oak and certain wheat.

Geography and terrain are also reflected in the climate. The hilly parts of the north are substantially cooler than the south. Winter snows in the Serra da Estrêla (which includes Portugal's highest peak at 1,986 meters) and the Serra do Gerês near the northern Spanish border may block roads for a period. The weather on the northern shores and in the heart of the nation is warmer; Lisbon has an average high temperature of 14°C in January and 27°C in August. Southern Portugal is warmer. The water moderates' coastal temperatures, although the interior of the Alentejo may be rather warm, with temperatures occasionally surpassing 40°C during the summer months. Due to its Mediterranean climate, most of Portugal's rainfall occurs in the winter, with the north getting far more rain than the south.

Portugal has ten significant rivers, five of which have their sources in Spain. The Río Minho originates in Spanish Galicia and for a distance of seventy-four kilometers constitutes the northern Portuguese boundary with Spain. The River Douro is of major significance to the trade of northern Portugal. It likewise begins in Spain and runs the whole breadth of Portugal until emptying into the Atlantic at Porto, the country's second biggest city. The Rio Douro is navigable by small vessels over its whole route of 198 kilometers in Portugal; traditionally the river was utilized to convey barrels of port wine to Porto. Its high banks are terraced with vineyards, and the valley of the River Douro is one of the most scenic in entire Portugal.

The Río Tejo is the country's longest river, has the greatest drainage basin, and is the most significant commercially. It is accessible just eighty kilometers upstream, although that includes the enormous estuary on which Lisbon is built. The Tejo estuary is the greatest natural harbor on the European continent and is equipped to accommodate huge ocean-going boats. It also houses the Cacilhas drydocks, the biggest in the world.

The most significant river in the south is the Río Guadiana which, running north to south, forms part of the boundary with Spain. Other notable rivers in Portugal include the River Lima and the Río Tâmega in the north, the Rio

Mondego in the middle, and the Rio Sado and Rio Chança in the south.

The soil systems of Portugal are mainly sandy, dry, and acidic, mirroring the soils of the Iberian Peninsula generally. The soil in the north might be rough. Northern Portugal is more adapted for agriculture than the south because of ample rainfall, although with sufficient irrigation the south could sustain more intensive agriculture.

However, one-fourth of Portugal is covered by forests which consist of primarily pine and deciduous oak; if such cultivated tree crops as olives, cork oak, almonds, chestnuts, and citrus are considered, roughly one-third of the country's land is tree covered. In the northern highlands, pine, oak, poplar, and elm trees are widespread. Vegetation is more diversified in the middle area and includes citrus trees and cork oak. The warm, dry south features several sections of rough grassland, as well as plentiful cork oak.

Furthermore, to mainland Portugal, the country's territory also includes the Azores and

Madeira islands. The Azores consist of nine inhabited islands and many uninhabited rock outcroppings 1,280 kilometers west of the mainland in the Atlantic Ocean. The archipelago has an area of 2,278 square kilometers with a population of roughly 250,000. The Azores generate adequate foodstuffs for domestic use and some exports, but they remain much more impoverished than the mainland. The Madeira archipelago, situated approximately 560 kilometers miles west of Northern Africa, comprises two inhabited and numerous uninhabited islands. With a total size of 788 square kilometers and a population of around 270,000 people, the archipelago is dangerously overpopulated.

Art and Architecture

Taking in Portugal's immensely diversified architecture requires going into the past as you look across medieval monasteries, magnificent hilltop castles, and ancient ruins.

From the beautiful castles and cathedrals of the Middle Ages to the distinctive modernist architecture of the 20th century, Portugal boasts a diversity of architectural styles.

The architecture of Portugal dates back to the Iberian Peninsula in the 5th century when Visigothic and Romanesque styles were utilized in the construction of churches and other religious structures. In the 12th and 13th centuries, Gothic architecture was imported to Portugal and may be seen in the cathedrals of Lisbon and Evora.

The Renaissance era witnessed the creation of the Manueline style in Portugal, a unique blend of Gothic, Renaissance, and Moorish elements. The Manueline style may be observed in many of the castles, churches, and monasteries that were created during this period, such as the Jeronimos Monastery in Lisbon.

Throughout the 19th century, Romanticism and Neoclassicism were fashionable in Portugal. This may be observed in the numerous large buildings that were created during this period, such as the Belem Tower in Lisbon.

Throughout the 20th century, Portugal underwent a phase of modernism. Architects such as Fernando Tavora, Alvaro Siza Vieira, and Eduardo Souto de Moura embraced modernity and developed some of the most unique and significant works of architecture of the period.

Portugal's rich architectural past can still be observed today in its cities and villages. From the elaborate cathedrals and castles of the Middle Ages to the modernist architecture of the 20th century, Portugal is a nation with a diversified and distinctive architectural history

Castles

It appears as though every Portuguese town with more than a handful of citizens has its castle. The Romans, Visigoths, Moors, Knights Templar, and Catholic kings all picked Portugal as home to their famed hilltop fortresses—and many of those castles still exist. Some have been turned into magnificent hotels, while others are bare remnants of the battlements they once were. Constructed over a millennium ago, they allow travelers to wander around their ramparts and into their decaying walls, on a ramble back in time.

The greatest series of Portuguese castles exist atop the low mountains that create a natural border with Spain: from Mertola in southern Alentejo to Miranda do\sDouro and Bragança in the country's northeast corner. Others dot Portugal's main cities, from Lisbon to Porto.

Unlike in France or Germany, most of Portugal's castles are rustic and unrestored. Local tourism offices give maps of walking routes around several castles and opening hours and entrance rates for the ones that you may visit. Be careful to remain within allotted borders, and keep youngsters near. They'll love the fairy-tale environment, although portions of the ramparts may be shaky.

Suggested Castles

Castelo de Almourol: Legend has it that this majestic fortress on an island of in the River Tejo is haunted by the soul of an old princess. Having Celtic and Roman origins, the castle was reconstructed by the Knights Templar in 1171.

The only way to visit is via boat, affording beautiful vistas along the route.

Estremadura and the Ribatejo Castelo de Marvão: This castle atop a mountain on the fringe of the settlement of Marvão has possibly the most stunning site of any in Portugal, with views of the São Mamede national park and the border with Spain. The castle walls swell with revelers during Marvão's celebrated chestnut festival each November.

Évora and the Alentejo Castelo de São Jorge: Atop Lisbon's tallest hill, this fortress has afforded the best views over Portugal's city for more than 1,000 years. Originally erected in the 6th century, the Castelo de São Jorge can single-handedly chronicle Portugal's history, and shaving has been held by the Romans, Visigoths, Moors, Portuguese kings—and /or snow by visitors from across the globe.

Castelo dos Mouros: All that's left of this 9th-century Moorish fortification is its outer walls, which provide one of Portugal's greatest rampart treks. Atop the castle walls, there are superb views of Sintra's second castle, the Palácio da Pena, and the Atlantic Ocean.

Palácio da Pena: A UNESCO World Heritage Site, this ethereal, pastel color palace in Sintra is one of the greatest architectural manifestations of over-the-top 19th-century Romanticism. It's a favorite among youngsters and those still young at heart.

Pousada da Rainha Santa Isabel: One of the few completely renovated castles in Portugal, this Estremoz fortification contains one of the country's best pousadas.

After pushing out the Moors, Portugal's ruler selected this hilltop fortress as his seat of authority. It's named after his wife, Queen Santa Isabel, who lived and died here.

Islands

Portugal is endowed with a breathtaking assortment of islands, from the isolated Azores in the Atlantic Ocean to the wild beaches of the Algarve coastline. But if you're seeking a place that delivers the finest of all these islands, the top and greatest island in Portugal is Madeira.

Madeira is an autonomous province of Portugal situated in the Atlantic Ocean near the coast of Morocco. The island is regarded to be one of the most beautiful islands in the world and provides a unique combination of both land and marine sports. From lush green mountains to crystal blue lakes, the island is a wonderland of natural beauty. Visitors to Madeira may experience some of the greatest hiking routes in Europe, discover the bustling city of Funchal, or just relax on the beautiful beaches.

In addition to its natural beauty, Madeira is a popular destination for its world-class restaurants and lodgings. From luxurious resorts to quaint cottages, the island provides a broad choice of lodging alternatives to suit all budgets. The island also features a busy nightlife, with a variety of pubs, clubs, and entertainment venues.

Lastly, Madeira is widely recognized for its superb wine. The island produces some of the greatest wines in the world, and tourists may taste a range of local wines and spirits.

In conclusion, Madeira is the top and greatest island in Portugal for people searching for a unique and amazing vacation experience. With its amazing natural beauty, exciting nightlife, and outstanding wine, Madeira is an island of heaven.

Chapter 2

Exploring hidden gems of Portugal

In recent years, the cities of Lisbon and Porto have been the choice destinations of tourists from over the globe and have been witnessing the biggest tourism boom in Europe. If you have previously had the opportunity to visit these two outstanding cities and wish to think beyond the box, come and experience some of Portugal's finest hidden gems.

These are among the most picturesque villages of Portugal or the most beautiful hidden sites of Portugal. Frequently hidden, and little known to vacationers, they are truly treasures and well worth a visit.
From the island of Farol through Casa do Penedo and the island of Flores, come and discover outstanding locations in one of the most beautiful nations in Europe.

Exploring lesser-known Locations

Portugal is one of my favorite locations in the world. It offers a variety of magnificent beaches, fantastic castles, exquisite wines, and some amazing villages that still keep their beauty and traditions.

Every visitor who picks Portugal as a destination knows about Lisbon, Porto, or Algarve, but Portugal has a lot more to offer than these renowned cities. If you're prepared to walk off the main track, you'll uncover some stunning sites still unknown to most visitors.

In this tour, I'll share with you the most gorgeous hidden jewels in Portugal that should be on every traveler's bucket list. Let me show you how different and wonderful Portugal is!

1. **Berlengas Islands, Leiria**

One of the most stunning secret destinations in Portugal, the barren and mountainous islands of Berlengas are wonderfully lovely. Situated adjacent to the town of Peniche, they include robust seagull colonies, as well as various types of birds and abundant marine life.

The highlight of this little rocky archipelago may be found on the main island of Berlenga Grande, where the historic fort of Sao João Baptista lies on a small rocky outcrop reached by a stone bridge. Aside from viewing the fort, you can also ride a boat or a canoe around the islands to find amazing caverns.

2. **Porto Moniz, Madeira**

One of Portugal's hidden locations, Porto Moniz is an extraordinary destination, nestled on the northern end of Madeira Island. The genuine marvel and the major appeal of Porto Moniz are the unique lava pools produced by the rising tide, where tourists may rest in one of the most intriguing landscapes.

These black basalt pools are suitable for swimming and are a fantastic location for people searching for a unique experience. If you wish to spend a longer time in the region, consider one of the hotels situated directly on the coast. You may visit this fascinating site with a guided excursion from Funchal. Check out this top-rated trip that includes visits to Cabo Girao, Paul da Serra, and more.

3. **Buracas do Casmilo**

The magnificent Buracas Valley is situated in central Portugal, close to the city of Coimbra and the town of Casmilo. The attraction boasts spectacular caverns and karst formations developed over millions of years along a small ravine that may be explored on foot.

It is one of the undiscovered spots in Portugal, a destination where you appreciate the beauty of nature without worrying about throngs of people. For anyone enthusiastic about geology and not simply, this is a must-see.

4. **Piodao**

There are many interesting sites in Portugal that people don't know about and one of them is the picturesque town of Piodao. This remote tiny village is nestled along a high mountain range, surrounded by woods and river valleys.

The densely packed dwellings are carved out of a rock called schist, providing an ideal scene that resembles a fairytale in the center of the mountains. Aside from enjoying the traditional ambiance while wandering on the small cobblestone streets, you should also see the white Parish Church.

5. **Covao dos Conchos**

One of the alternative things to do in Portugal, Covao dos Conchos is quite bizarre, seeming almost like an extraterrestrial doorway. Situated in the heart of an artificial lake in the isolated Serra da Estela Mountains, this sinkhole is an artificial funnel.

It goes into an underground tube that is part of a hydroelectric system that delivers water to local settlements. There are no other constructed buildings around and the hole seems nearly natural.

6. **Monsanto**

Several years ago, this historic community was selected as “the most Portuguese village in Portugal” and much of its charm has been retained to this day. Those who prefer to experience Portugal off the usual route should surely visit Monsanto, a little community nestled deep in the countryside close to the Spanish border.

The typical granite buildings were erected amid massive rocks that are part of the rural scenery itself, being incorporated into the dwellings. The tiny streets are likewise paved with stone. If you have enough time, see the intriguing remnants of an ancient castle and church at the top of the hill.

7. Costa Nova do Prado

One of the most spectacular Portugal hidden treasures is the coastal location of Costa Nova do Prado, situated near the town of Aveiro. Brightly colored vacation houses are situated along this gorgeous beach. They were created by fishermen and used as storage in the past.

Situated on a long length of beach between the ocean and a lagoon, this unique spot is a paradise for surfers and those who enjoy the untamed side of Portugal's coast.

8. Sao Miguel Island

This lovely destination's moniker is "Green Island" owing to the lush woods surrounding mountain peaks and turquoise lakes produced in past volcanic calderas. The biggest island in the Azores Archipelago is an astonishing site where everything seems like a postcard, from the spectacular shore sculpted by the Atlantic Ocean to the twin blue-green lakes at Sete Citades.

Among the most attractive features on this island are a few thermal baths, cities with a rich cultural past, and spectacular panoramic views that can be enjoyed from the mountain peaks. You may also go whale watching or explore the wonderful western half of the island with a guided trip.

9. Obidos

The little village of Obidos is situated in the Oeste Region and is one of the hidden spots in Portugal. Situated on top of a hill and encircled by ancient walls, the town has a towering castle and stunning medieval architecture, as well as an alluring ambiance.

The primary highlights of Obidos are the well-preserved castle, the typically painted buildings, the blossoming lanes, many spectacular churches, and interesting festivals. There are also wonderful beaches situated on the shore nearby.

You may visit Obidos as a day excursion from Lisbon. This top-rated trip also includes stops at other amazing destinations such as Fatima, Batalha, and Nazare.

10. Terceira Island

The third biggest and second most inhabited island of the Azores is also known as the "Lilac Island". This lush and paradisiac resort has amazing unspoiled beaches and wonderful tiny villages in the center of nature.

Yet, the attractions of Terceira are the inspirational hiking pathways leading to amazing sites like the Algar do Carvao lava tunnel or the Serra de Santa Barbara Peak. The vistas are just spectacular! I suggest arranging a guided tour of the island like this one to see as much as possible of this destination at an inexpensive price.

11. Ponta do Bode Madeira

Situated on the western side of Madeira Island, this spectacular little rocky peninsula is one of the undiscovered locations in Portugal, a genuinely lovely area with amazing views of the dramatic coast of the island and the ocean.

Situated near the town of Canical, it's worth visiting especially for the spectacular sunset vistas. While in the region, you may also visit the magnificent natural beauty of the Canical Peninsula.

12.Marvao

The medieval treasure Marvao is one of the greatest unique things to do in Portugal, delivering an exciting experience deep in the countryside. The ancient castle of Marvao rises on a steep ledge above the stunning whitewashed stone homes and picturesque cobblestone lanes of the medieval town.

With its tumultuous past owing to the vicinity of the Spanish border, the town of Marvao is best renowned for its castle, but it also boasts a modest museum, various hiking pathways, and other fascinating views nearby.

13.Amarante

Situated in the countryside far north, the lovely town of Amarante is one of the less-known destinations in Portugal. Situated at the foot of the mountains and crossed by the lovely

Tâmega River, the town rests on many hills and is surrounded by woods.

The principal sites of this historic destination are the Sao Goncalo Bridge, the São Goncalo Church, the Museum of Modern and Contemporary Art, the Santo Domingos Church, and the Aquatic Park. If you decide to visit this town, plan a day excursion to the Serra do Marao Mountains.

14.Coimbra

One of the most undervalued cities in Portugal, the picturesque city of Coimbra is typically disregarded in favor of Lisbon or Porto, although it provides the same amazing experiences. Currently a flourishing academic city, it was formerly the medieval capital of Portugal.

Apart from one of the oldest universities in the world and a vibrant cultural life, Coimbra also features several exceptional attractions, including the Old Cathedral and the New Cathedral, the Botanical Garden, the Santa Cruz Church, the Machado do Castro National

Museum, the Portugal dos Pequenitos theme park, and many others.

15.Braganca

Situated in the far northeastern tip of the country, the ancient village of Braganca is one of the most intriguing locations in Portugal. Its superbly maintained medieval castle with thick stone walls surrounds the town.

Braganca is a remarkable find, containing various fascinating things to visit such as the Medieval Castle and the Military Museum, the historic Domus Municipal structure, the Old Cathedral, the Santa Maria Church, and the old town area with attractive alleyways and workshops.

16.Tomar

Tomar city Portugal

Situated amid the nation, the town of Tomar is incredibly magnificent. Back in the 13th century, this was one of the most prominent and powerful towns in Western Europe. It used to be the religious headquarters of the Knights Templar.

The Convent of Christ was their major temple and it's still the most renowned site in Tomar, but there are many other great things to view, such as the Tomar Castle, the Pegoes Aqueduct, Sao Joao Baptista Church, or the picturesque old town area.

17.Braga

One of the oldest towns in the nation, Braga is one of the strangest locations in Portugal. Regarded as the religious hub of Portugal, the city is home to outstanding churches and monasteries, such as the Bom Jesus Church, the Old Cathedral, the Santa Cruz Church, the Our Lady of Sameiro Sanctuary, and others.

Additionally, numerous museums, parks, and palaces are waiting to be found. Braga is also one of the greatest sites to enjoy the traditional "green wine", often known as "young wine".

18.Cascata das 25 Fontes, Madeira

The magnificent 25 Fontes Waterfalls are extremely amazing. Situated in the rugged interior of Madeira, these falls may be explored via a trekking trail, passing through some amazing landscapes. The spectacular Cascata do Risco is nearly 100 meters high but the others are as wonderful, compensating by their distinctiveness or beauty.

19.Beach da Adraga

Considered one of the most gorgeous beaches in Portugal, Beach da Adraga is situated near Lisbon. The major lure of this wild and picturesque beach is the spectacular towering cliffs that descend into the water, providing a breathtaking panorama. It has wonderful golden sand and there is a nice restaurant at the entrance, where you can have a delicious dinner.

20.Sortelha

One of the oldest and finest preserved medieval towns in the nation, Sortelha is one of the forgotten locations in Portugal. With its spectacular castle built on 760 meters high rock and its ancient granite buildings that stand between stones and rocks, this little village provides an amazing rural excursion in eastern Portugal.

Learning from Experiences

Visiting Portugal will be just as fantastic for you as it was for me. I believe that with the planning suggestions and guidance I have in this book, together with the valuable and inspiring knowledge about this lovely nation, you will be well on your way to becoming a seasoned expert at traveling from Alentejo to the Algarve to Lisbon with ease. I will give you suggestions on what to pack and prepare for before you go, teach you about the cuisine, the art, and the environment present in each place, as well as provide you with useful phrases from the charming Portuguese language. So rest assured; you are in good hands and it will be a holiday you will be delighted you spent money on.

Portugal Nightlife: Bar and Club

Taking a visit to Portugal and ready to make the most of the country's excellent nightlife is important. And here are some of the top venues for Portugal's nightlife.

The Algarve

Being one of Europe's most popular summer vacation destinations, the Algarve is famed for its lively bars and clubs and continues to draw many British visitors all year round. In the summer, it's not only one of the greatest regions for nightlife in Portugal, but it's also one of the top partying destinations in all of Europe.

Lagos, Albufeira, and Praia da Rocha are popular destinations for partying, while the resorts of Quinta do Lagos, Vale do Lobo and Almancil are recognized for their up-scale nightlife and luxury hotels. From romantic pubs to stag-themed party venues and beach clubs, there's something for every taste in the Algarve.

Faro, the capital of the Algarve region, is also renowned for its dynamic student-themed

Portuguese nightlife because of the enormous number of students studying in the city at the University of Algarve. If you're staying in Vilamoura, a favorite base for honeymooners, you'll discover lots of beautiful cocktail bars and high-end venues near the resort's luxury harbor.

Lisbon

Compared to the crowded beach resorts of the Algarve, the Portuguese capital offers a considerably more realistic vibe. You'll find over 100 pubs and restaurants in the Bairro Alto district, one of the primary centers of nightlife in Portugal, however, if you prefer a partying environment, go to venues like Urban Beach, Lux, or Plateau, which are situated in other regions of the city. Several pubs in Lisbon remain up until at least 3 am, while discos or clubs typically don't shut until 6 am when it's already light in the summer.

Porto

This ancient port in the north is the nation's second city and has grown more famous among clubbers, owing to its bohemian Portuguese nightlife. The core of Porto's nightlife is in the downtown area, where pubs and clubs get quite packed at weekends, however, you may find calmer bars in the Passos Manuel neighborhood if you'd like something more laid-back. The Industrial District is also renowned for its discos and commercial house music, while the old Ferreira Borges Market is a favorite party and concert theater.

Nightlife Tips

Nightclubs and bars in the Algarve are at their liveliest in the peak season, from June to September, when huge numbers of families, couples, and groups of friends enjoy their summer vacations. The Portuguese frequently eat pretty late compared to northern Europe, which is why many clubs don't start going until around 10 pm or 11 pm. Numerous clubs here stay open far into the early hours, and live entertainment such as comedy performances and concerts are commonly in English.

Take in mind that many nightlife establishments on coastal resorts in the Algarve will be closed outside of the peak season, however, this is a terrific opportunity to grab some amazing last-minute offers at very inexpensive rates and experience the calmer side of nightlife in Portugal.

Chapter 3

Before Trip Preparation

Before you decide to visit any country of your choice, you need to be aware of some vital trip tips and tricks to ensure that you have a safe and smooth vacation.

When to visit

Portugal is fantastic at any time of year provided you select your location correctly. In mid-summer, the coast is pleasant and bright, while interior parts bake till the grass is brown (reaching the 40C in the middle and south) (reaching the 40C in the center and south). June brings the bright São João celebrations, which are at their liveliest in Porto when residents smash each other over the head with rubber hammers and dance till dawn in the streets. Fall and winter are magnificent in the Serra da Estrela mountains — with golden leaf fall and ample snow for skiing. Madeira features among Europe's hottest, sunniest mid-winters. Spring is wonderful everywhere – particularly in the Alentejo and Centro areas, which are lush and blossoming with wildflowers. April and May are the greatest periods to watch Blue Whales in the Azores.

Best time to visit

Portugal is hot and bustling in mid-summer. Go in the shoulder seasons (April, May, and September) and you'll enjoy even better weather, and accommodation and restaurant rates will be up to 30 percent cheaper.

How to get there

The cheapest and fastest way to go to Portugal is on a budget aircraft into Lisbon, Faro (in the Algarve), or Porto. Although Brittany Ferries is exploring creating direct routes between the UK and Porto the only method to access Portugal by boat is now through Spain. Ferries run twice weekly from both Portsmouth and Plymouth for Santander (23 hours). Santander is a four to five-hour trip from the Portuguese border in Bragança. There are also direct buses from Santander to Porto, running roughly 10 hours - visit flixbus.co.uk.

Getting to and around Portugal

Portugal is modest - 350 miles long and roughly 130 broad – so there's no need to take internal flights. Although there is an excellent, frequent railway service (not high speed) connecting the coastal towns, interior places might be a problem to access on public transport - with few rail links and unreliable buses. The best method to get about is via rental automobile.

Portugal essentials

Whenever you travel in Portugal, utilize this useful checklist to make sure you don't leave home without those important goods.

1. **Passport or ID card:** Residents of the EU, Switzerland, Norway, Iceland, and Liechtenstein require simply a valid ID card. People from Canada, the US, South America, Australia, New Zealand, and most Asian countries going to Portugal need a passport only - no visa is necessary for stays under 90 days. Citizens from other nations should look here.

2. **Airline tickets:** If you have an e-ticket, print off the email confirmation just in case.
3. **Hotel reservations:** Having a printout may be handy for taxi drivers.
4. **Credit/debit cards:** Visa, Mastercard, and American Express are generally accepted. Bring an ATM debit card to withdraw euros from your bank account. In Portugal, ATMs, or Multibancos (MB), are simple to locate, at the airport, Lisbon, Porto, and even in little Portuguese villages.
5. **Driver's license:** You'll need one if you wish to hire a vehicle.
6. **Whatever medications you need:** If you go to a drugstore in Portugal, medicines may probably have a different name. Therefore, if there is something you can't live without - bring it with you.
7. **Toiletries:** Shampoo, shower gel, toothpaste, toothbrush, and don't forget your deodorant to keep fresh when visiting Portugal.
8. **Smartphone (with charger):** It has become necessary for most tourists since it contains everything – camera, guide book, map, wallet, etc.

9. **Camera:** Portugal is incredibly picturesque because of its light, scenery, and beautiful architecture. Carry a decent camera if you wish to have more power than your smartphone can supply.
10. **Sunglasses, hats, and sunscreen:** Particularly during late spring, summer, and early fall, the sun is quite intense in Portugal. Apply sunscreen on any exposed skin, even if you're not on the beach. Select a 30 SPF or more to protect you from sunburn, UV damage, and skin cancer.

Best things to do

Driving along the Spanish border

Spain is Europe's oldest contentious border. Littered with ancient walled cities and villages – constructed by Romans, Moors, Christian rulers, and British troops under Wellington – it's a fascinating trip. And the vistas of craggy mountains, heaths, river-cut canyons, and large lakes are stunning.

Stay in a remote pousada

Spain has its pousadas, Portugal its pousadas - old monasteries, palaces, and castles reborn as elegant country hotels. The country's interior is speckled with them – from the ancient Phoenician castle of Alcacer do Sal in the Alentejo (a hop from the fashionable beach at Comporta where Madonna has a home), to a converted convent next to the sprawling palace where a young Catherine of Bragança grew-up before leaving to become Queen of England.

Walk the Vicentina Coast

Cutting through wildflower meadows, cutting into secluded coves, and over cliffs nested by storks and peregrine falcons, The Rota Vicentina is one of Western Europe's prettiest coastal walks. You may spend a week or more strolling the full length – from Sagres at the southwestern edge of the Algarve to the enormous beaches near Sines in the Alentejo, or you can walk a tiny section in the morning or an afternoon.

Travel cost

You should prepare to spend roughly €109 ($119) per day on your trip to Portugal, which is the average daily price based on the costs of previous travelers. Previous tourists have spent, on average, €32 ($35) on meals for one day and €21 ($23) on local transportation. Additionally, the average hotel price in Portugal for a couple is €95 ($103). Hence, a vacation to Portugal for two persons for one-week costs on average €1,527 ($1,660). All of these typical travel rates have been gathered from previous travelers to help you plan your trip budget.

Best Hotels

The Algarve

By Spanish standards, Portugal's portion of the Mediterranean coast remains pristine. In pieces. True, there are cities of concrete condominiums, high-tower resorts, and golf courses, but there are wild expanses too. Silk-soft stands and rolling dunes extend for tens of lonely km surrounding Tavira Island in the east; while in the West, at Sagres, the coast crumbles into cave-pocked cliffs and crescent bays backed by butterfly-busy meadows. And then there are the hills, with their Mykonos-white homes and castle towns and their tiny spa villages – like Monchique, located in pine trees next to a gushing, clear-water stream.

The Silver Coast

With its terracotta cottages nestled around a clifftop above a long, golden beach, Nazaré doesn't seem like one of the world's adventure sports capitals. Yet in fall and winter, the world's most courageous surfers congregate here, to ride the world's greatest waves — hundred-foot-high rollers that smash into the shore. It's an astounding sight. And surfers lured here are learning that the community stands in the midst of one of Europe's prettiest beachfront locations — the Costa Dourada. It's stunning at any time. There are beautiful beaches of various kinds and sizes surrounding Nazaré, Peniche, and Aveiro (some tranquil enough for babies, others excellent enough for year-round championship surfing) and loads to do nearby. Travel a few miles inland to explore the historic hilltop university city of Coimbra, the little walled village of Óbidos (with its fantasy castle), and the towering Gothic Abbeys at Batalha and Alcobaça.

Madeira

Does Europe have a nicer island than this? Madeira's craggy mountains and rice-paddy-green terraces tumble to honey-colored beaches and a Caribbean-clear sea. Winding roads join little sugar-cube hamlets, paths that climb into the mountains, and a succession of cliff-top miradors with breathtaking sunrise and sunset vistas. Sea-cooled, Madeira's never too hot in summer. In winter it's warm enough to swim in the water. And in spring the landscape is bright with flowering oleander, agapanthus, and lilies of the valley

Azores

This mid-Atlantic island is Europe's Hawaii — a collection of beach-fringed smoking volcanoes set in an inky-blue ocean. There's wonderful hiking, mountain biking, and surfing and, with some of the purest air outside the poles, the sunsets and starry sky is beautiful. Yet it's the wild, unpolluted ocean that's the major lure. There's nowhere better in Europe to witness whales and dolphins - with an incredible 25 species visiting the Azores yearly, including the biggest mammal on Earth, the Blue Whale, which migrates here in spring.

The Alentejo

Extending across the bottom of Portugal between Lisbon and the Algarve, the Alentejo is Iberia's Tuscany (without the tourists) (without the crowds). Come for tranquil stone towns encircled with ancient walls and capped with castles; explore their tiny streets and happen upon a forgotten local café offering wonderful Alentejo wines, olives, and cheeses. Travel through meadows and down little roads to Roman remains and standing stones older than Stonehenge, and swim off uninhabited beaches backed by crumbling, caramel-colored cliffs.

Serra da Estrela mountains

The Serra da Estrela mountains – a 90-minute drive from the Silver Coast – have some of Portugal's loveliest landscapes: gorgeous gorges cut by rushing mountain rivers and stepped with waterfalls; steep valleys of tumbling terraced fields sitting at the feet of granite Hobbit-villages; and enough snow in January and February for a small ski resort.

Portuguese Cuisine and Drink to Try

Cataplana de Marisco

A journey to Portugal wouldn't be complete without ordering a mouth-watering dish of Cataplana de Marisco. Unique to the Algarve area but initially inspired by North African cuisine, this seafood stew with prawns, clams, fresh fish, ripe tomatoes, and seasonal Mediterranean vegetables, is steam-cooked in a copper clam-shaped dish that folds close. Savor this typical Portuguese lunch with a cool, fresh white wine overlooking the azure-blue seas of the Atlantic Ocean.

Grilled Sardines

Sardines have long been a popular catch in Portugal and, while shoals have reduced over the years, this fish remains a significant icon and favorite local cuisine, particularly in the Algarve. Sardines are traditionally grilled, dusted with salt, and served on a piece of rustic bread with a bit of lemon. The native technique to consume sardines is with your fingers, like an ear of corn, so no silverware is necessary and filthy fingers are ensured!

Piri Piri Chicken

A far cry from a fast grab-and-go lunch at Nando's, a typical Portuguese dish of Piri-Piri chicken is full of fresh spices and bold tastes. Spatchcocked chicken is marinaded in a handmade combination of garlic, olive oil, salt, lemon juice, and Piri-Piri chilies, before being cooked on the barbeque for a subtle charcoaled scent. Served with a fresh green salad, rice, or chips, you'll find this simple but spicy meal offered across Portugal.

Port

Port is a sweet fortified wine that is commonly enjoyed as an after-dinner aperitif or with a board of excellent artisan cheeses. Port wine comes from the beautiful vineyards of Portugal's Douro Valley, but it is in Porto that the crushed grapes are fortified with an aguardiente spirit, matured in barrels, and bottled. Visit a classic port lodge in the city to learn about the history and manufacture of white, ruby, and tawny port varietals and enjoy the varied flavors in a tasting session.

Pastéis de Nata

Kick back and watch the world go by at a chic Lisbon café as you dig into some of Portugal's famed custard tarts - Pastéis de Nata. These flaky pastry cups are filled with a delicious vanilla custard tinged with a touch of cinnamon, whipped to perfection, and nicely toasted. This delightful sweet delicacy may be served hot or cold but is best enjoyed outside with a smooth black coffee.

Chapter 4

Pre-Trip Preparation and Logistics

So, you've chosen to take the leap and commit to visiting one of continental Europe's most intriguing and beautiful countries—congratulations! You are no doubt quite thrilled to be traveling but, if you have gone overseas before, you will know that the run-up to the holiday is just as crucial (and thrilling) as the trip itself. [t is a time to get yourself organized and prepared to make sure that your time away works well and you are not left with any unpleasant surprises when you return. So here are a few things, based on my personal experiences, you should do to aid. After all, "you fail to plan, you are intending to fail" (Benjamin Franklin).

Buy Tickets Early

My first recommendation is to schedule your flight or other means of travel, as early as you can. You could feel a little nervous about committing too far in advance, but there are perks for both of you in the facility you select to leave from. For instance, booking early helps airports and airlines to plan for passenger numbers and minimize disasters or difficulties with Logistics, which is why certain flights are accessible to purchase around a year before the departure date. This will also provide you with a feeling of stability and enough time to organize everything else, including trips, time off work, and childcare, for example.

Naturally, a year in advance may be too early for many some us, particularly if to want to acquire possible last-minute offers but waiting too late might lead to full disappointment or even make incur expensive costs, so there is an art to achieving the correct balance. According to Advance Aviation, considerably shorter journeys. passengers should start researching flights a month or before their intended travel date, but for foreign journeys, travelers Can consider booking up to five or more months in advance, particularly if they •want to travel during busy seasons (Sourwine, 2022). (Sourwine, 2022). Peak periods are when there is a significant demand for transportation, such as during holidays and summer or spring vacations, as many people will want to utilize their time off work or school to visit friends and family or are just in need of some time away to decompress.

If going to Portugal is highly costly for you, reserving early might make paying for it simpler also since many travel companies permit payment in installments. For example, you may only be needed to pay as little as $80 to ensure your ticket on a flight. paying the balance monthly until a month before you are supposed to go. This may make it simpler for you to manage your funds over time and not have the worry of putting together a huge lump amount and perhaps losing out on vacation possibilities entirely.

If you are traveling as a group. reserving your accommodation early is also a smart idea as you will be more likely to acquire rooms in the same hotel or apartment complex. You could even have a higher probability of acquiring upgrades! Booking early may also guarantee you have enough time to make previous arrangements with the hotel if you need any particular amenities, as the more warning they have, the more likely it is for them to be able to accommodate you.

For example, if you are pregnant, have mobility challenges, or are traveling with persons with special needs, informing them early can offer hotels more time to ensure that you are allotted rooms that are a short walking distance from the entrance and exits or have an elevator or slope access.

Inform Friends and Family

Unless your vacation to Portugal is a surprise to people traveling with you or those who reside in the country, notifying loved ones where you are going, what hotel or apartment you will be staying in, and for how long is a very good idea. This will provide you and their peace of mind, so that if you were to need any help while overseas, they know just where to locate you. They'll also be more likely to be able to provide help in your absence if you give them an adequate warning. So if you need pet care, need your plants watered, or need the bins carried out on a certain day, let others around you know that you'll be gone and could do with some assistance as soon as you can.

Advising trustworthy neighbors when you will be on vacation is also good for your home security, as they will be able to check out for any strange behavior in addition to your security systems.

Protect Your Apartment

Safeguarding your house and assets while you are gone is crucial. After all, your vacation is transitory, but your house is your foundation and is no doubt extremely dear to you, therefore caring after it at this time should be one of your priorities.

Here are a few recommendations that will assist you to keep it safe and ready for your return.

i. Don't post about your trip on social media. As tempting as it is, try not to publicize that you will be away from home, particularly if you live alone or if your whole household will be coming with you.
Sadly, this may give burglars the green signal to visit your home and you might wind up with a bad surprise on your return. Instead, defer publishing images and videos publicly until you come back and only share with individuals you trust.

ii. Make your house look occupied. If the movie Home Alone has taught us anything, it is that making your house look as though there are people in it can be a deterrent to thieves! An empty home with the mail or deliveries piling up, an empty drive, and no lights on at night can all, unfortunately, draw their attention.

iii. Double-check that you have locked your windows Aa and doors. This sounds very obvious, but you would be amazed at how many people forget to close a window or leave a back door unlocked when leaving for vacation. Unfortunately, this can be a costly mistake and invalidate some home insurance policies if the worst was to happen. So check, check, and check again!

iv. Hide any valuables from plain sight. [f you can, move your computers, laptops, and jewelry away from view through any windows, or better yet, lock them away in a home safe. Safes are a good investment, but if you don't have one, tucking items under the bed or behind a closed internal door should be enough.

v. Get an alarm system. If you haven't already got one installed, having an alarm system is a great way to scare away burglars and instantly notify the police of any break-ins. If you are unable to get one before going away, there are some smart signs and deterrents available online which look very convincing!

vi. Turn off water and unnecessary electrical devices. You should not only protect your home from theft, but also from damage, and that includes flooding and fire. Before you leave, if you are going to be gone for quite a while, it might be wise to turn off your water supply from the source as this can protect you from any unexpected leaks. You should also unplug any gadgets or devices, such as televisions and washing machines that would normally be on standby. Being on standby still burns electricity, so there is also a small chance that they could be a fire risk if they overheat. By switching devices off completely, you'll also have the added bonus of saving money.

Notify Your Provider

Those that need to know that you are leaving the nation include your bank and mobile phone carrier. This is because if you use your card to pay for anything overseas without alerting them, certain banks may detect this and flag it as suspicious account activity. This might lead to your access and card being denied, and nobody wants this while purchasing a beverage at a beach bar! Your bank may also charge for overseas transactions, therefore it is good contacting to them ahead of so that you are aware of their rules and may make additional arrangements if need be.

Your mobile phone network operator should also be addressed for similar reasons as you wouldn't want to be charged inadvertently and extortionately to make or receive calls while utilizing a foreign network. Alternatively, they may be able to give you an international "roaming" package, which will be cheaper and safer for you to use your phone while in Portugal.

Get Insured

Buying travel insurance as soon as you book your flights and accommodation is a prudent thing to do. It will prevent you from losing a huge amount of money if any unexpected circumstances lead you to miss or cancel your trip, whether it is your fault or not. Insurance would also offer you financial protection if something was to happen to your health in Portugal. For example, if you are an adrenaline seeker and adore watersports, you should consider obtaining insurance just in case the jet ski ride around the marina doesn't exactly go to plan. Additionally, if you have any pre-existing medical issues, insurance will be able to pay for any urgent care or medicines you may require while outside of your own country. You'll also be able to cover any valuable things like iPads, computers, or cameras that have the potential to be lost or stolen. Therefore, urge that everyone should obtain a decent level of travel coverage, for a piece of mind and added personal security.

Safety and Health

All COVID-19 travel restrictions have been lifted for entrance into Portugal, except for those for travelers coming from China. In hospitals, nursing homes, and other healthcare settings of today environmental situations face masks are necessary. The COVID-19 community transmission rate is still high. Portugal's winter months may see localized floods, especially in metropolitan areas. Keep an eye on the media and heed the guidance of regional authorities.

Safety

Bag Snatching, pickpocketing, and auto theft are all common crimes. Keep expensive items hidden.

Beaches, tourist destinations, and public transportation are places to be mindful of for your personal property safety and security. The police have received reports of violent assaults related to pickpocketing. There are violent crimes including robberies and assaults. Another concern is the spiking of drinks.

Avoid accepting beverages from random people or leaving unsecured drinks.
Be on the lookout for lodging frauds. They are increasing. Utilize official websites to make hotel reservations.
On the beaches of Portugal, people get drown on some beaches of Portugal, and always Follow the instructions of the lifeguard. A red sign Always do indicate danger; and that's a notice or sign you should refrain from entering the water. Watch out for warnings concerning cliff erosion when needed.
While strolling in urban areas, be mindful of the typical Portuguese pavement. The mosaic stone pavements may be hazardous, particularly when it rains. Severe harm could happen. Avoid walking on the slick pavement by staying off of the roadways; doing so might lead to severe collisions with vehicles, trams, and bicycles.
In the summer, bushfires often affect mainland Portugal. Keep an eye on regional media and heed the suggestions and directives of regional authorities.
Portugal's winter months may see localized floods, especially in the cities. Keep an eye on

the media and heed the guidance of regional authorities.

Itinerary Planning Guide

Avoid making the same mistake I did! Be sure to do your homework and schedule as many of your outings as advance as you can. This will not only help you make sure you can visit all the places you want to in your limited time, but it will also help you save time and money. For instance, consider paying for transportation to go through the picturesque regions of the Douro Valley in northern Portugal without learning that the area is also home to beautiful wineries, museums, and vintage trains. When you could have done two things at once, you didn't have to pay for a second journey to the same location to see these sights. Make two lists: one of all the locations you would want to see but it wouldn't be the end of the world if you didn't, and another one of all the sites you couldn't leave Portugal without having visited. This will make your planning simpler.

After you have them organized by location and know how long each activity will take, you can schedule your days so that the "must-sees" get the most attention. By planning your trip in this way, you'll also find it easier to pack your clothes. For instance, if you only want to visit the beach occasionally but lots of museums, volcanoes, and historic towns, you'll know to pack just one or two sets of swimsuits but lots of comfy shoes and casual but stylish clothing. Since you would want to be certain of the precise time, location, and mode of transportation you would be taking to and from Portugal, without the need for an internet connection, having your flight itinerary printed out and having it with you may also be extremely helpful. If the Wi-Fi at your hotel went down when you needed it and you couldn't access your flight information, it would be awful.

Hire a vehicle

While traveling, renting a vehicle might provide you greater flexibility to explore Portugal once you are there. Traveling by own vehicle is a smart decision if you want to see the whole nation or just like your own space, since public transportation may be congested and challenging if you aren't familiar with the stops and linkages. But, if you're staying in a crowded, touristy city like Lisbon or Porto, you may not need a vehicle to get about since there are so many accessible transportation choices. There are clean, effective, and user-friendly trains, trams, buses, taxis, and funiculars available.

Since you won't have to worry about getting lost, renting a vehicle in Portugal may also allow you the option to choose accommodations that are a bit farther off the usual path. After you leave the cities, you'll notice that people tend to drive slower than the posted speed limit, therefore accidents are less common. It is safe and easy to drive there.

Just keep in mind that Portuguese drivers prefer to drive on the right side of the road, parking can be challenging at times, you'll need to purchase adequate insurance, and nearly every new highway in Portugal now has an electronic toll system. Weigh all of your options before deciding to rent a car. If you do decide to, I advise booking it before you arrive in Portugal so you don't lose out on one of the sizes and kinds you want. An insider's recommendation is to hire your vehicle from Lisbon rather than, say, the Algarve since the

Algarve's rental rates often increase during peak travel times.
So which kind of vehicle should you choose? However, I'd think that a little economy vehicle is good, even for a family, since driving a big car through tight curves, blind corners, and cobblestone streets may be stressful! Also, you should choose to walk the last few kilometers rather than park in historic city centers. Also, avoid mindlessly following your GPS since it may sometimes recommend steep, dangerous bypasses if you are inexperienced with the terrain.
Overall, renting a vehicle is a fantastic alternative that, if used carefully, may lead to more adventure, experience, and opportunity.

What to pack

When you dust out your luggage and start fetching your old Euros from the attic box, you know it's time to start packing for your holiday! Packing can be both thrilling and stressful, so I've put up a checklist of goods you should bring so you can enjoy your once-in-a-lifetime vacation to Portugal without feeling like you've forgotten anything!

Needless to say, regardless of where you are going, you should always bring the following with you.

1. For obvious reasons, your passport is.
2. Travel documents, such as your travel schedule, insurance paperwork, and emergency contact information. Preferably, items should be printed rather than shown on an electronic device.
3. Money. Not just for your time away, but also for spending at your home airport, meals, and, if necessary, transportation cost back home.

4. Any regularly prescribed medicine you take, as well as anything else you believe you may need while abroad, such as an Epi-Pen, stomach settling tablets, migraine meds, and so on.
5. Toiletries such as toothbrushes, toothpaste, lotions, shower gel, shampoo, deodorant, and so on.
6. A selection of clothing and undergarments appropriate for your area and activity plans, plus a few extras!
7. Pajamas or other nightwear that is both comfortable and cool.
8. An excellent book or pastime to keep you entertained while resting in your accommodation or on the beach.
9. Sunglasses, a sturdy sun hat, sunscreen, and everything else you need to be safe from the elements.
10. Swimwear. Even if you're not a great swimmer, it's recommended to carry a

wetsuit with you for activities like boat rides or lagoon dips.

More to Pack-Clothes, Shoes, and Accessories

1. A couple of additional clothing for either chilly or warmer weather.
2. Handbags or backpacks are OK. Waterproof phone cover.
3. A high-quality camera.
4. If you're going alone, bring a selfie stick.
5. A water bottle that can be refilled.
6. A simple first-aid kit.
7. Earplugs and an eye mask are recommended.

Portugal has a variety of climates, ranging from the chilly temps of Porto in the north to the sunnier climate of Tavira in the eastern Algarve. Thus, even if you believe you'll be staying on the sunny beach every day, carry a scarf, shawl, or waterproof clothing. You never know how strongly the Cálem wine tasting in Porto may appeal to you, and you don't want to be put off coming because of your lack of clothing. But, if you are staying in colder places, a pair of light t-shirts and shorts wouldn't hurt; in fact, layers are always better, so you can strip down if necessary!

A waterproof phone cover may also be handy since the breathtaking Portuguese vistas do not stop at sea level! Many snorkeling opportunities may be found just off the continental shore. Although the cooler temperatures and stronger currents make snorkeling more difficult than in the Mediterranean, if you are a confident swimmer with snorkeling or diving experience, you won't want to miss out on capturing the seabed life in Praia do Camilo or Praia da Marinha, which are located between Portimio and Albufeira.

If you like great photography, don't forget to bring your camera since there are some magnificent landscapes that most phones just cannot capture. For example, Aveiro is regarded as "the Venice of Portugal" because of its gorgeous canals, nouveau architecture, and colorful gondolas, or the harsh mountainous environment of the Parque Natural da Serra da Estrela, Portugal's oldest and biggest protected natural area (Pettit, 2022).

I also suggest packing baggage that can be securely tied since, despite Portugal being one of Europe's safest nations (third out of 163), it is always prudent to be cautious (Jennings, 2020). Pickpocketing is one of the most often reported crimes in Portugal, therefore carrying a well-fastened bag that does not catch too much attention could help to lessen this danger. You may even invest in a money belt, avoid wearing expensive-looking jewelry, and always put your purse on your lap or in front of you when eating at restaurants. Bags that may be worn on your back (or front) can also come in helpful, particularly if you plan to travel across uneven terrain and need both hands free to maintain your balance.

Ear plugs and eye masks can also let you sleep in the early afternoon or have a lie-in in the morning if you decide to travel during busy festival periods and stay in a popular neighborhood.

Budgeting, Money, and Currency

The escudo was the Portuguese currency before the introduction of the money in 1999. Euros and cents are now recognized in the majority of EU nations, making it simpler for non-European tourists. While visiting Portugal, you should bring both cash and a card, since the nation is generally cash-centric, particularly outside of Lisbon and Porto. With this in mind, my advice is to always carry small euro notes or a few one or two euro coins with you since smaller stores, cafés, or pastelaras may struggle to accept higher quantities; even a €20 bill. If you do decide to use your card despite this, keep in mind that you may be charged for overseas transactions by the seller or your bank, so always check ahead of time.

Portugal is regarded as the most affordable nation in Western Europe due to its lack of tourism. Drinks, including alcohol, seldom cost more than two or three euros, and a restaurant supper, even at the most formal establishments, rarely costs more than €50 per person, so why not treat yourself to a big meal at a local restaurant on your first and final days?

Clothing and shoes

Please take my advice and keep in mind that cobblestone streets may be found practically wherever in Portugal! Calçada Portuguesa is a sort of mosaic floor that adorns numerous pedestrian areas, so bring comfortable flat shoes to prevent any painful falls on your strolling excursions. This sort of terrain may also be a bit slippery, therefore when paired with hills and steep slopes, you should wear non-slip soles. You don't have to wear full-on hiking boots everywhere, but it's not worth it to explore these places in wedges or thin heels.

Maps

Packing a good old-fashioned Portuguese paper map is usually a smart idea, particularly if you won't have access to a local phone with data or a solid internet connection. You may seem to be a tourist, but that is preferable to get lost in the heart of the Mercado Santana market with no clue how to get back to your flat!

Adapter with portable charger

In Portugal, your hotel room will most likely have one of two plug types: type C or type F. Plug type C has two round pins and plug type F has two round pins plus two earth clips on each side, both of which run on 230V supply voltage and 50Hz, thus you will most probably need to acquire an adapter if your country of origin has a different plug type. Bring a portable charger with you for those lengthy all-day outings or when you've spent too much time relaxing by the pool!

This guide

Last but not least, you must carry this book with you! Put it in your carry-on or bag to refer to as and when you make your way around the nation, and learn a few Portuguese words along the way! With this book, you'll be able to explore any place from the Alentejo area to the Algarve and Madeira islands with confidence and appreciate the culture, cuisine, and people that come with them.

Chapter 5

Best Churches in Portugal

1. Ermida de Nossa Senhora da Lapa (Vieira do Minho)

The Chapel of Nossa Senhora da Lapa [Our Lady of the Cave], erected in the 60s of the last century, is situated near the Gerês, on the Penamourinho hill, in the Soutelo parish. It stands out for the fact that it was erected within a cave on a big hill and used to be one of the most significant shrines in Europe.

Tradition has it that the Virgin Mary appeared to a young shepherd girl. The devotion led to pilgrimages that spurred the building of the modest church.

2. Bom Jesus do Monte Shrine (Braga)

This National Monument and UNESCO World Heritage Site in Braga stands out from other churches in Portugal owing to its remarkable surroundings and construction.

The Bom Jesus do Monte is a Catholic Shrine and architectural landscape setting that comprises a church, a wide staircase that acts as a Way of the Cross, and even a forest. The location prompted the creation of the Nossa Senhora dos Remédios Shrine in Lamego.

Among the features is the Latin cross-shaped Basilica, one of the earliest neoclassical structures in Portugal, as well as the spectacular stairwell, separated into three flights: the portico stairs, the stairs of the five senses, and the stairs of the three virtues of faith, hope, and charity.

3. Santo Ildefonso Church (Porto)

The Church of Saint Ildefonsus, or Santo Ildefonso, in Porto, is an example of the aesthetic skill that dominates the bulk of Portugal's churches. Rebuilt in the first part of the XVIII Century, the façade is formed of two bell towers with cornices and its walls are covered in tiles painted by Jorge Colaço, portraying episodes from the life of Saint Ildefonso.

Features include the rococo altarpiece in baroque gold plate and the neo-classical side altars.

4. **Senhor da Pedra Church (Vila Nova de Gaia)**

About 12 kilometers outside of Porto, on the Miramar beach in Gulpilhares, you'll discover the extraordinary Senhor da Pedra Chapel [Lord of the Rock], that on hazy mornings appears to hover above the sand.

Raised in 1686 on a rock directly by the seashore, its beginnings lay in a pagan religion that flourished among the pre-Christian people who worshiped their Gods in the natural.

The temple would eventually be converted to Christianity, keeping the attractiveness of its site and giving birth to one of the most traditional pilgrimages in Vila Nova de Gaia.

5. **Saint Marinha da Cortegaça Church (Ovar)**

Academics think that this church goes back at least to the mid-XII Century. It is noted for its stunning blue and white tiles symbolizing St. Peter, St. Paul, Saint John Bosco, Saint Francis of Assisi, the Sacred Heart of Jesus, and the Heart of Mary that line the architecturally rich and ornamented cathedral. The church's façade is regarded as one of the most stunning in Portugal.

6. Batalha Monastery (Leiria)

Also known as the Santa Maria da Vitória Monastery, it was established in 1386 by D. João I, Master of Avis, in thanksgiving to Our Lady for the triumph against the Castilians in the Battle of Aljubarrota.

It belonged to the Order of Saint Dominic and was only completed in 1563, being a superb example of Gothic architecture in Portugal, has been listed as Unesco World Heritage, and named after one of the Seven Wonders of Portugal in 2007.

7. São Domingos Church (Lisboa)

The São Domingos Church, situated near the Rossio, in Lisbon, stands noteworthy for its baroque and mannerist design. It was also made renowned by the Royal Weddings which took place there, as well as the calamities that happened.

Constructed in the XVIII Century, it survived the 1755 earthquake but was seriously damaged in a catastrophic fire in 1954 that destroyed not only a significant portion of its structure but also the gold-plate ornamentation and numerous paintings.

After the fire, it was not entirely repaired, which creates a lasting effect on visitors. It was subsequently recognized as a national monument. The interior is rich and diversified, with massive columns ornamented with marble and tiles.

8. Estrela Basilica (Lisboa)

This historic Catholic house of worship used to be a Carmelite monastery and was established in the second part of the XVIII Century, after a pledge between Queen Mary I and D. Pedro III over the birth of a new born son. It was the first church in the world to be consecrated to the Sacred Heart of Jesus and the Queen herself is buried there.

It distinguishes noted for its conclusion of the baroque era and neoclassic styles, the dome, and the Machado de Castro statue in the façade.

The use of marble on the interior is remarkable, as are the tones of grey, pink, and yellow that shimmer in the sunshine that pours in through the dome.

The remarkable Machado de Castro nativity scene, comprised of over 500 cork and clay figurines, only comparable to museum artifacts, is another reference in this cathedral which stands out from other Portuguese churches for many reasons.

9. Jerónimos Monastery (Lisboa)

Commonly known by the name Santa Maria de Belém Monastery, this national icon was established in the XVI and has been a UNESCO world heritage site since 1983. In 2007 it was designated as one of the seven wonders of Portugal.

It marks the height of Manueline's design and is certainly the most significant monastic edifice of its epoch in Portugal, regarded as one of the primary salon churches in Europe.

Features include the south and west-facing doors that should be considered as a diptych, carved in tribute, and to the glory of, King D. Manuel I.

10.Brazilian Evangelical Church in Portugal

Established in 1879 by mathematician and engineer Miguel Vieira Ferreira, the Brazilian Evangelical Church was instantly acknowledged by the Imperial Government and attracted members of the elite classes of Rio de Janeiro.

Based on confidence in the direct revelations of God and the influence of the Holy Spirit, it naturally found its way to Portugal through the years.

Best Parks and Gardens in Portugal

Portugal is a gorgeous nation with a panorama of lush valleys, rolling hills, and kilometers of coastline. Its parks and gardens are a monument to its beauty and charm, providing tourists an opportunity to see the country's natural splendor in all its splendor. From enormous gardens to breathtaking parks, Portugal offers something for everyone. These are 10 of the nicest parks and gardens in Portugal.

1. Park Eduardo VII, Lisbon: Parque Eduardo VII is the biggest urban park in Lisbon, comprising 40 hectares. The park provides a variety of activities including walking, running, bird viewing, and cycling. It is also home to a variety of plants and trees, making it a fantastic area to relax and appreciate the beauty of nature.

2. Parque Natural da Serra da Estrela, Viseu: Situated in the Serra da Estrela mountain range, this park is an excellent spot to enjoy the natural beauty of Portugal. It is home to a diversity of flora and animals, including rare kinds of birds, and provides tourists with lots of chances to trek and explore the region.

3. Jardim Botânico da Ajuda, Lisbon: This gorgeous botanical park is situated in the center of Lisbon and encompasses an area of 6.5 hectares. It is home to a variety of plants, trees, and flowers, and is a terrific location to relax and appreciate the beauty of nature.

4. Jardim do Ultramar, Porto: Situated in the city of Porto, Jardim do Ultramar is a magnificent park with amazing views of the Douro River. The park is home to a variety of trees and plants, as well as a lake and a fountain. It is a terrific area to relax and take in the splendor of the city.

5. Parque Desenvolvimento Urbano, Faro: This park is situated in the city of Faro and is an urban paradise. It is home to a variety of trees, plants, and flowers, and provides tourists with plenty of chances to stroll, run, and cycle.

6. Parque Natural Sintra-Cascais, Lisbon: Situated just outside of Lisbon, this park is a terrific site to discover the natural beauty of Portugal. It is home to a variety of flora and trees and provides tourists with lots of chances to walk, ride, and enjoy the spectacular vistas.

7. Parque Natural do Tejo Internacional, Lisbon: Situated along the banks of the Tejo River, this park is a terrific site to enjoy the natural splendor of Portugal. It is home to a

variety of flora and trees and provides tourists with lots of chances to walk, ride, and enjoy the spectacular vistas.

8. Parque Natural do Ria Formosa, Faro: This lovely park is situated on the shores of the Ria Formosa lagoon. It is home to a variety of flora and trees and allows tourists lots of opportunities to explore the region.

9. Jardim do Palácio de Queluz, Lisbon: Situated in the city of Lisbon, this lovely garden is home to a variety of plants and trees, and allows tourists an opportunity to take in the breathtaking views of the city.

10. Parque Natural da Arrábida, Setúbal: Situated in the Arrábida mountain range, this gorgeous park is home to a variety of flora and trees, and allows tourists lots of chances to explore the region.

Best Galleries in Portugal

When it comes to art galleries, Portugal is no exception. These are the top 10 greatest galleries in Portugal that you should visit in 2023:

1. The Calouste Gulbenkian Museum- Situated in Lisbon, this museum includes a permanent collection of approximately 8,000 pieces of art, including paintings, sculptures, and sketches. It also displays temporary exhibits presenting art from all across the globe.

2. The Berardo Collection Museum- This museum is situated in Cascais and is home to a rare collection of modern and contemporary art from the 20th century.

3. The National Museum of Ancient Art- This museum is situated in Lisbon and has one of the most significant collections of Portuguese art from the 15th to the 19th century.

4. The Arte Institute- Situated in Lisbon, this museum is devoted to modern art and showcases both national and international artists.

5. The Serralves Foundation- This museum is situated in Porto and is home to an excellent collection of modern and contemporary art.

6. The Serralves Museum of Contemporary Art- This museum is situated in Porto and is home to a vast spectrum of modern and contemporary art from throughout the globe.

7. The National Museum of Modern Art- This museum is situated in Lisbon and includes one of the greatest collections of modern and contemporary art in Portugal.

8. The Azulejo Museum- This museum is situated in Lisbon and is devoted to the history and art of the traditional Portuguese tile.

9. The Museum of Modern Art- This museum is situated in Lisbon and includes one of the greatest collections of modern and contemporary art in Portugal.

10. The National Museum of Decorative Arts- This museum is situated in Lisbon and has an excellent collection of decorative art from the 16th to the 19th century.

With so many excellent galleries to see, Portugal is a terrific vacation for art lovers and aficionados. Whether you're seeking a unique collection of modern and contemporary art or a fascinating glimpse into the history of ornamental art, Portugal has something to offer everyone.

Best Places to Eat in Portugal

1. The Yeatman Hotel, Porto

With two Michelin Stars, The Yeatman is one of the top restaurants in Portugal. Its dining area overlooks Porto's Ribeira neighborhood, fleets of servers cater to you and the seafood-tasting menu is superb. Enjoy delicacies like sea urchin or tuna and turbot.

Every meal is complemented with exquisite wine and the restaurant's cellar is famed.

2. Mini Bar, Lisbon

Mini Bar, Lisbon is one of the top restaurants in Portugal. Michelin-Star restaurants in Michelin-Star restaurants in Lisbon don't come better than Mini Bar managed by Michelin-Star chef José Avillez and hidden within Art

Deco Theatre de São Luis. It provides a correspondingly dramatic cuisine, so consider seaweed ice-cream cones stuffed with tuna tartare or ‘exploding’ olives.

Each entrée is delivered in a sequence of unforgettable 'acts', another dramatic homage to the restaurant's location. And if you want to hang out after dinner, Bairro Alto is the greatest neighborhood to stay in Lisbon for nightlife.

3. Midori, Penha Longa, Sintra

Japanese Midori was the first ethnic restaurant in Portugal to be granted a Michelin Star and you'll find it in Sintra. Select a seven or nine-course tasting menu for delights like mackerel tataki with crispy tomato and gazpacho, turbot with bell pepper nasu dengaku, and smoked tuna nigiri.

Always save space for sake jelly after dinner and ponder about spending overnight in World Heritage Sintra. It sits on our list of finest things to do in Portugal and is also the most visited destination in the whole country.

4. Rei das Praias da Caneiros, Algarve

Travel to Portimão off-season and the odds are you'll have lovely Beach da Caneiros to yourself. You won't be able to miss Rei das Praias, the restaurant on stilts, directly on the beach. It's an elegant establishment, despite the unusual design, and offers the most exquisite Algarve seafood.

Start with oysters or clams in garlic sauce then move on to delicious fish roasted in salt or opt for fish cataplana - seafood soup created in a big wok.

5. Choupana, Vila Nova de Milfontes, Alentejo

In Portugal location alone may make a restaurant remarkable. Go to Choupana in Vila Nova de Milfontes as evidence. When the tide’s up here, you're at one with the Atlantic. Waves surge against the waterside terrace. The catch of the day is grilled outdoors, on a barbecue.

Sunsets on the side of this restaurant are magnificent also and it's easy to understand why Alentejo is featured as the greatest location to dine.

6. Taberna da Rua das Flores

Situated in Lisbon, this traditional restaurant serves a broad assortment of Portuguese food, such as codfish, octopus, and pig. The ambiance is comfortable and the service is friendly.

7. A Cozinha, Porto

Situated in Porto, A Cozinha provides a unique combination of traditional Portuguese and Spanish food. The menu is always changing and contains specialties such as hog confit and seafood stews.

8. Belcanto, Lisbon

Belcanto is a Michelin-starred restaurant that provides a unique combination of Portuguese and French cuisine. The tasting meals are widely praised, and the ambiance is elegant but welcoming.

9. Pote, Lisbon

O Pote is a historic restaurant that specialized in seafood. The menu contains a range of foods, from grilled octopus to fish stew.

10. Restaurante Largo, Faro

Restaurante Largo specializes in traditional Portuguese food. The menu comprises meals like pig stew and grilled sardines, as well as a range of local wines.

11. A Tasquinha, Lagos

A Tasquinha provides a large range of classic Portuguese meals. The menu contains delicacies such as grilled sardines and pork stew, as well as a range of marine dishes.

12. Taberna do Mercado, Lisbon

Taberna do Mercado is a historic restaurant that specializes in Portuguese food. The menu contains several seafood delicacies, such as grilled octopus and fish stew.

13. Restaurante O Afonso, Lisbon,
Restaurante O Afonso is a Michelin-starred restaurant that serves a unique combination of traditional Portuguese and French cuisine. The menu comprises items such as hog confit and seafood stews.

14. A Tasca da Rua, Porto
A Tasca da Rua is a classic restaurant that specializes in Portuguese food. The menu contains delicacies such as grilled sardines and pork stew, as well as a range of marine dishes.

15. A Perola do Bolhão, Porto
A Perola do Bolhão is a historic restaurant that specializes in Portuguese cuisine. The menu comprises meals such as grilled octopus and fish stew, as well as a range of local wines.

Entertainment and Nightlife

Portugal has become one of Europe's most popular vacation destinations. It features some of the world's greatest beaches, wonderful history, magnificent architecture, fantastic cuisine, and of course, great nightlife. You can find a nice night out anywhere around the nation, but some are always going to be better than others. From traditional Fado locations to multistorey superclubs, these are seven of the greatest places to go in Portugal for nightlife and entertainment.

Top Best Places to Go in Portugal for Nightlife

1. Lisbon

The country's capital has to be one of the top spots to go to in Portugal for nightlife. The city is a dynamic center of art, culture, music, gastronomy, and of course, amazing nightlife. Although Lisbon draws tourists, hosting roughly 3.6 million visitors each year, it's one of the greatest locations to experience living like a native. The most popular region is the Bairro Alto District. Commonly regarded as Lisbon's party quarter, it's fully crammed with bars. Most of them are very tiny, so you'll see the celebrations spilling out into the streets, people jumping from one pub to another, creating an almost nostalgic ambiance. Bars are performing a diverse spectrum of music, from jazz to live DJs. And to get a flavor of true Portugal, come to Tasca do Chico for a live

Fado (a distinctly Portuguese genre) performance every night from 8 pm.

It may become fairly congested on the tiny streets, particularly during the summer months. Make a beeline for one of Bairro Alto's numerous rooftop bars, such as Zé dos Bois and Insólito. Normally, people start in this area before traveling to Cais do Sodré. With the biggest number of disco bars and late-night clubs in the city, there's no lack of places to go. Some of the greatest commercial clubs are Roterdão Club, Rive Rouge, and Titanic Sur Mer. If you want something a little more laid-back and a bit different, Pensão Amor is an unusual pub — it's a former brothel and still has the old entrance. Sol e Pesca is a former fishing store that keeps the same décor, while Crafty Corner offers you the very finest Portuguese craft beer.

2. Porto

Although Lisbon is wonderful for partying like a native, Porto comes out on top for that. Porto is growing appeal with visitors, but it's still pretty local. The nightlife here is diverse, ranging from inexpensive little pubs to sophisticated cocktail venues. Foz do Duoro is the place to go if you appreciate premium beach bars, watching the sunset, and enjoying the ambiance. There are a few nightclubs here, but it's largely popular amongst individuals searching for a mellow atmosphere. If you appreciate easygoing and refined nightlife, Porto offers an excellent and distinct wine culture. You'll discover many port buildings along the Duoro River, providing tastings of port and other wines. No vacation to Porto is complete without attending a port tasting. After all, the cocktail was called after Porto!

If you're looking for more of a party, go to Galerias de Paris. This street, as well as Cândido dos Reis and Conde de Vizela, are the core of Porto's nightlife. Similarly, to Lisbon, the celebration tends to spill out into the streets. It's relaxing yet has a fantastic vibe, with most people bouncing from one bar to the other. If you want to go to clubs, there are several wonderful alternatives — Base is a renowned open-air club, Piano B is for house music enthusiasts, and Boîte offers everything for everyone.

3. Lagos

Lagos is the Algarve's surfing town. While you're here, you'll hear a lot of Australian accents. It's built for a highly entertaining, vibrant, and inexpensive nighttime environment. There is a significantly younger audience here, but there's something for everyone. In line with the surfer and backpacker ethos, go to Joe's Garage, MJ Bar, The Star, Legends Bar, The Lionheart, or Three Monkeys Bar. Although there's largely a pub feel in Lagos, the celebration continues till the early hours at Grand Café. It's pretty much the closest thing to a club in Lagos, and most people wind up here at the end of the night. And although it may seem like a party town (which it is), it's hardly Magaluf level. The pubs are in interesting old buildings, with friendly bar staff that'll come to identify you after a few evenings.

Lagos is as popular with families as it is with travelers. The pubs are by no means backpacker-exclusive, and several small wine and cocktail bars suit those searching for a relaxing ambiance far better. Tannins, for example, offers an outstanding assortment of wine and dishes up to wonderful Mediterranean cuisine. For a combination between a vibrant environment and superb drinks, make a beeline for Bon Vivant. The unusual structure boasts a popular rooftop terrace, the ideal site for partaking in everyone's favorite past-time, people-watching.

4. Albufeira

The Algarve is packed with locations to go for nightlife in Portugal, all providing something a little different. Whether it's a traditional Lads' Holiday or a Lady's Holiday that you're wanting, Albufeira is the spot for you. It's renowned as the Algarve's primary party town, particularly popular with visitors. Streets are lined with neon signs, stag, and hen parties, and if you needed any more proof, the main strip for nightlife is simply named The Strip. There are too many bars to list, but if you start here and see where the night leads you, you're guaranteed to have a fantastic time. And if you're seeking to dance the night away at a club, the most popular are Club Paradise, Club Vida, and Liberto's.

It isn't all late-night partying in Albufeira, either. If you prefer something a little more low-key, the marina is a great area to watch the sun go down with a good drink in hand. It's also bordered by tapas bars, so you can munch on olives, drink wine, and admire the vista of superyachts and catamarans.

5. Faro

Faro is substantially more laidback than other cities in the Algarve. Yet that isn't to suggest there isn't a vibrant nightlife scene here. It has a significant student population; thus a lot of the nightlife is based around them. Mainly, Faro's busy party culture develops around Rua de São Pedro, Rua Conselheiro Bívar, and Rua do Prior. Youth masses rush out into these streets, which are packed with laughter and music. There's plenty to appeal to every musical taste here and because of the student population, the drink costs are relatively inexpensive. Thursdays tend to be the largest night out here owing to, you guessed it, the student population!

If you walk farther into the Old Town, you'll discover lots of smokey wine bars, quiet cocktail places, and jazz bars. Havana Club is one of the city's greatest cocktail bars, offering up Caribbean-inspired drinks and putting on sophisticated music concerts. And if jazz is your thing, go to Manoel's Jazz Club for some seductive melodies.

6. Vilamoura

If you haven't realized by now, the Algarve, in general, offers amazing nightlife. Nonetheless, Vilamoura is arguably the most diversified. There's a nice mix of trendy pubs, cosmopolitan cafes, nightclubs, sophisticated wine bars, and upscale beach clubs. Most of them are around the Marina, where you'll find bar after bar. If you appreciate the finest things in life, come to the elite Bond Club. It's one of the most upscale clubs in the Algarve, dishing up innovative cocktails and local wines. For a smokey, eccentric feel, you should visit the Cave. It's dark, dreary, and mysterious. Another popular restaurant is Botequim; it's more of a laid-back atmosphere, with couches, lo-hi music, and elegant, contemporary surroundings.

Quarteira is an area just outside of Vilamoura, that's popular with Albuferia and Vilamoura residents as well as visitors. It's home to multistorey megaclubs that pound out music till the early hours. Discoteca Lick and BLISS are two of the most popular, and greatest, locations to party till the sun rises.

7. Coimbra

Alright, Lisbon and Porto are wonderful tourist places for partying like a native. Yet, if you truly want to fit in with the locals, consider a vacation to this gorgeous university town. Far less recognized than the other venues on our list, we promise you'll be friends with everyone in the pub by the end of the night. With its student population, a lot of the nightlife does focus around them, but there's also so much authenticity to experience in this quaint town that's earnt a status as one of the greatest locations to go in Portugal for nightlife. Enjoy Fado music at traditional taverns, such as Diligencia Bar, where the customers often take up the guitar themselves.

One of the most popular pubs in town is Bar Quebra Costas, situated between the medieval old town and the downtown area. It’s set on a hill and by night, people flood out into the sloped cobblestone streets, chanting local folk tunes. If you’re eager for dancing the night away at a discotheque, you’ve got lots of possibilities. Pinga Amour is a local favorite, TUTTI is your typical student club, and if rock music is your thing, you’ll enjoy Noites Longas.

Best Places to Stay

Depending on the kind of visitor you are and the kind of experience you want, there are many different places you may stay.

Although being a small nation on the Iberian Peninsula, Portugal is nonetheless a destination worth visiting. It is, especially if you wish to savor exquisite wines, gaze at stunning coastal vistas, and stroll through medieval cities' cobblestone alleys. You'll undoubtedly need a place to stay. Fortunately for you, Portugal offers some amazing hotels to go along with its attractions. You may choose between staying in more contemporary castles with rooftop patios and infinity pools or historic ones, perhaps one encircled by Moorish walls. All of these accommodations in Portugal, whether they are simple or elaborate, give the charm that the nation is known for.

1. Portimao's Bela Vista Hotel and Spa

The Bela Vista Hotel and Spa in Portimao, which was built in 1918, has extravagantly beautiful decor—even the grand piano is decorated with artwork. It was more akin to a castle than a family house when it opened as the Algarve's first hotel in 1934. You'll want to take in the scenery from a lounge chair or the pool while perched on a hilltop overlooking the ocean. While the public spaces are lavishly decorated on every square inch, the suites have more subdued design elements that promote rest.

2. Hotel Six Senses Douro Valley

When you stay at Hotel Six Senses Douro Valley, you'll experience what it's like to be a manor born. The hotel is housed in a grand manor home from the 19th century that has views of the Douro river and valley. The hotel is four hours from Lisbon and has a rustic yet modern ambiance inside. A sense of tranquility is enhanced by forests, undulating hills, and vineyards. Given that the Douro Valley is one of the oldest wine-producing regions in the world, the hotel has a wine library where local winemakers give demonstrations.

3. Lisbon's Hotel Avenida Palace

The ancient neighborhood of Lisbon is home to the Hotel Avenida Palace, which represents a piece of the city's past. It is housed in a neoclassical structure from the 19th century that exudes old-world elegance. The interior maintains its appeal with vintage furniture that captures the luxury of the time. The Hotel Avenida Palace is a five-star luxury hotel with excellent reviews from customers who have used it. Some rooms have subdued decor, while others have bright striped bedding, wall coverings, and drapes. The bathrooms are marble in every room.

4. Madeira's Estalagem da Ponta do Sun

Consider staying at the Estalagem da Ponta do Sun, a hotel that is perched on a cliff overlooking the ocean, if you want to get away from it all. This hotel, which is situated on Madeira, offers its visitors a distinctive stay by fusing a modern structure with an antique "Quinta" or farmhouse. There is nearby surfing, scuba diving, and whale watching, as well as a 500-year-old hamlet to visit if you grow bored swimming in the heated indoor pool or the infinity pool. The apartments are furnished simply and include balconies or patios.

5. Lisbon's Memmo Alfama Hotel

The Memmo Alfama Hotel, which is situated in the heart of the historic area, maybe a good option if staying in the center of Lisbon is vital to you. From the rooftop terrace and wine bar, which look out over the River Tagus, to the first-floor wine bar and pool, this 42-room boutique hotel exudes elegance. This adults-only hotel, which is housed in a late 19th-century structure close to Lisbon's most important historical landmarks, was recognized as one of the year's best new urban hotels.

6. The Pousada do Castelo in Obidos

When you stay at the Pousada do Castelo, a historic castle from the ninth century, in the walled city of videos, you may act like a king.

The historic structures and antique furniture in the public spaces remain even if the hotel is now contemporary. The Pousada do Castelo, one of Portugal's seven wonders, was built as a wedding gift for a king and queen who wed here in 1282. Several of the inner walls have not changed much throughout the years.

7. Santa Barbara Eco-Beach Resort

It doesn't get much better than that: your villa with a view of the sea or mountains, palm palms swinging in the breeze. The first modern resort in the Azores is Santa Barbara Eco-Beach Resort, which is situated on San Miguel Island. The resort is a great spot to surf because it views the well-known Santa Barbara surfing beach. You can also observe whales from the resort or just relax by the ocean-facing pool. Breakfast is either provided as part of the tariff or can be prepared in your kitchenette.

8. Belmond Reid's Palace

A historic hotel that has been delighting its visitors for 125 years is called Belmond Reid's Palace. Three swimming pools are the first thing in this, one of which has hot seawater in it. The resort is surrounded by lush subtropical gardens and is perched on a cliff overlooking the Atlantic Ocean in Funchal, on the island of Madeira. Families are welcome at Belmond Reid's Palace, and children are welcomed with a teddy bear. Moreover, there is a playhouse for children and a soundproofed technology area for teens.

9. Montemor-o-L'AND Novo's Vineyards

You'll certainly like staying at L'AND Vineyards in remote Altenjo if you want to see the night sky. There are retractable roofs in certain rooms, allowing you to stargaze in solitude. The hotel is situated next to a lovely lake, while Montemor-o-Novo, a medieval village, is located across the lake. Visitors who want to bike along the lake can borrow bicycles from L'AND Vineyards. Modernist in design, the interior has hand-woven carpets that were manufactured in the area. The hotel's restaurant, which serves wines from the hotel's vineyard, holds the only Michelin star in the area.

10.Hotel Bussaco Palace

Maybe as a result of Portuguese King Charles, I'm construction of the Bussaco Palace Hotel in 1888, it has an opulent palace-like appearance. The monarch intended to construct Belem Tower in Lisbon but was surrounded by a forest. The hotel is situated in the Bussaco woodland not far from Coimbra. Guest rooms are furnished in early 20th-century styles, and the interiors are adorned with antiques and artwork. The hotel strives to emphasize elegance rather than contemporary amenities, therefore the rooms lack air conditioning but do have telephones and satellite TV.

11.Porto's The Yeatman

The Yeatman, a premium hotel in Porto, offers the most breathtaking views when breathtaking scenery is a requirement. The hotel has a view of the Douro River and Porto, which at night is dazzlingly illuminated. Day or night, a rooftop terrace with a lounge and a pool is a terrific spot to take in the city. The accommodations are distinctively furnished; perhaps you'll be assigned to a room with a bed encased in a massive wine barrel.

Best Ways to go Around

Portugal is walkable. During a short stay, probably, you won't use any public transportation (other than coming into town from Campanhã station or the airport), that's when you arrive at Porto, —unless you prefer to go for a historic trolley joyride.

1. The easiest method to travel to Portugal is to hire a vehicle. Hiring a vehicle provides you the freedom and flexibility to explore Portugal at your leisure. You may also make pauses and diversions along the trip. Additionally, you don't have to worry about having to wait for public transit or dealing

with the bother of navigating foreign public transportation systems. Additionally, with a vehicle, you can explore many of Portugal's more isolated and less popular locations, which is perfect for those who want to see a more real side of the nation. Moreover, automobile rental businesses in Portugal usually provide affordable pricing and frequently give rental packages that include extra amenities such as GPS navigation systems and liability insurance.

2. you may take the train. Portugal’s rail network is vast and efficient, serving most of the main cities and villages in the nation. Riding the train is typically the most pleasant and convenient method to travel since the country’s trains provide comfortable seats, air conditioning, and baggage storage. Additionally, rail rates are generally lower than flights and vehicle rentals.

3. you may ride the bus. Portugal's bus network is enormous and covers much of the nation, which makes it a wonderful alternative for those who wish to see the country on a budget. The buses are typically pleasant and dependable, and you can sometimes obtain cheap rates if you book in advance.
4. you may take a cab or hire a private driver. Hiring a cab or hiring a private driver is a terrific way to go to and from the airport or to tour the city. Taxi rates may be pricey, so it's important to settle on the amount before getting in the taxi.
5. you may hire a bicycle. Portugal is an excellent nation for cycling, and you can simply hire a bicycle in most cities and towns. It's a terrific opportunity to experience the nation on your terms, and it's also a great way to keep active and healthy while on vacation.

6. you may take a ferry. Portugal offers a variety of ferry lines that link the mainland to the islands, and this is a terrific way to see the country's coastal areas. The boats are typically pleasant, and you can frequently obtain cheap rates if you book early.
7. you may take a tour. If you don't want to bother about the logistics of traveling throughout the nation, you may always elect to join a guided tour. Tour companies provide extensive packages that include the key sites and attractions of Portugal, and they also provide transportation and lodging.
8. you can take a flight. Portugal's largest cities are linked by air, and this is a terrific method to move across the country swiftly and efficiently. Domestic flights are frequently cheaper than international ones,

and you may often get reduced rates if you book early.

9. you may take a boat. There are a variety of ferry and boat routes that link the mainland to the islands, and this is a terrific way to see the country's coastal areas. The boats are typically pleasant, and you can sometimes obtain cheap rates if you book in advance.

Eventually, you can hitchhike. Hitchhiking is a terrific way to travel to Portugal on a budget, and it's also a great opportunity to meet people and experience the country more realistically. It's crucial to apply common sense while hitchhiking and to make sure that you're not placing yourself in any unsafe circumstances.

Chapter 6

Holidays and Festivals Celebrations in Portugal

January:

One of the most prominent holidays held in Portugal in January is the Feast of the Epiphany, which is commemorated on January 6th. This festival recalls the day that the three wise men visited the newborn Jesus. On this day, children get presents and families gather to eat traditional Portuguese foods. Another notable event in January is the Day of the Kings, which is observed on the Sunday before the Feast of the Epiphany. This day honors the three wise men who visited the newborn Jesus. On this day, the family meets to eat a traditional cake with a trinket within.

February:

In February, one of the largest events in Portugal is Carnival. This carnival takes place in the cities of Porto, Lisbon, and Madeira. During this festival, parades, celebrations, and street dances take place around the country.

Participants dress up in colorful costumes and masks, and the celebrations linger for many days. Another notable event in February is the Feast of Our Lady of the Candles, which is observed on February 2nd. This holiday pays tribute to the Virgin Mary and is celebrated with processions and joyous dinners.

March:

In March, Portugal commemorates the feast of Saint. Joseph. This day is devoted to the patron saint of Portugal and is celebrated with processions, feasts, and fireworks. On this day, families gather to eat traditional Portuguese feasts that include delicacies like Caldo Verde and stewed fish. The events also feature traditional dances and music. Another notable festival in March is Good Friday, which is commemorated on the Friday before Easter Sunday. On this day, several churches organize special services and guests are welcome to attend.

April:

April symbolizes the beginning of spring in Portugal, and with it comes numerous major holidays. The most prominent of these is the Easter holiday, which is commemorated with religious services, processions, and special dinners. Another notable festival in April is the Feast of Saint. George, which takes place on April 23rd. This day is devoted to the patron saint of Portugal and is commemorated with parades and religious rituals.

May:

In May, one of the important holidays in Portugal is Labor Day. This day is commemorated on May 1st and is a public holiday. On this day, many workers and union members take part in parades and protests to highlight the significance of labor rights. Another notable event in May is the Feast of the Ascension, which is held on the 40th day following Easter Sunday. This day marks the ascension of Jesus into heaven and is commemorated with religious services and processions.

June:

In June, Portugal commemorates the feast of Corpus Christi. This event takes place on the Thursday after Trinity Sunday and is celebrated with processions, feasts, and unique activities. On this day, churches and chapels are decked with flowers and decorations, and families assemble to share traditional feasts. Another notable event in June is the feast of St. Anthony, which is commemorated on the 13th of June. This day is devoted to the patron saint of Portugal and is celebrated with processions, dances, and music.

July:

In July, one of the biggest festivals in Portugal is the Feast of Saints. Peter and St. Paul. This day is commemorated on the 29th of July and is a public holiday. On this day, churches host special services and processions, and families assemble to eat traditional Portuguese cuisine. Another notable event in July is the Feast of Our Lady of the Mountain, which is observed on the 15th of July. This day is devoted to the

Virgin Mary and is honored with processions and joyous banquets.

August:

In August, Portugal commemorates the Feast of the Assumption. This is a public holiday that is observed on the 15th of August and is devoted to the Virgin Mary. On this day, churches organize special services and families assemble to eat traditional Portuguese cuisine. Another notable event in August is Port Wine Day, which is celebrated on the 4th of August. This day is dedicated to the manufacture and consumption of port wine and is celebrated with processions, celebrations, and music.

September:

In September, Portugal commemorates the feast of Saint. Michael the Archangel. This day is commemorated on the 29th of September and is a public holiday. On this day, churches host special services and processions, and families assemble to eat traditional Portuguese cuisine. Another notable event in September is the Feast of Our Lady of Mercy, which is observed on the 24th of September. This day is devoted to the Virgin Mary and is honored with processions and joyous banquets.

October:

In October, Portugal commemorates the feast of Saint. James. This day is commemorated on the 25th of October and is a public holiday. On this day, churches organize special services and families assemble to eat traditional Portuguese cuisine. Another notable holiday in October is the Feast of Our Lady of the Rosary, which is celebrated on the 7th of October. This day is devoted to the Virgin Mary and is honored with processions and joyous banquets.

November:

In November, Portugal commemorates the feast of All Saints Day. This day is commemorated on the 1st of November and is a public holiday. On this day, churches organize special services and families assemble to eat traditional Portuguese cuisine. Another notable event in November is the Feast of Our Lady of the Immaculate

Conception, which is observed on the 8th of November. This day is devoted to the Virgin Mary and is honored with processions and joyous banquets.

December:

In December, Portugal commemorates the feast of the Immaculate Conception. This day is commemorated on the 8th of December and is a public holiday. On this day, churches organize special services and families assemble to eat traditional Portuguese cuisine. Another notable festival in December is the Feast of Christmas, which is observed on the 25th of December. This day is devoted to the birth of Jesus and is celebrated with processions, songs, and celebratory banquets.

Portuguese Words and Phrases

Considering a vacation to Portugal? Don't forget to learn a few basic Portuguese phrases and words before you leave! It's extremely vital to learn some basic words in the local language for any trip, as it's a terrific way to show respect to the people and improve your travel experience. Portuguese is a wonderful Romance language but it might take time to get the hang of it, so start with some basic but fundamental words/terms like greetings, and please, and thank you. To assist you on your journey, here are 15 fundamental Portuguese phrases to master before your vacation to Portugal.

1. Hello – Olá

Get off to a good start by welcoming individuals with "olá" (hi or hello) (hi or hello).

It's one of the most crucial but fundamental Portuguese words to learn and you won't go far without it!

2. How are you? - Cómo está?

After you've said olá or bom dia, follow it up by adding "Como vai?" (how are you?). If someone asks you this question, you may answer with a simple "bem" (well) or say "eu estou bem" (I am well) (I am good). If you wish to inquire how they are too, add "E tú?" (and you?).

You may also use “tudo bem?” or “tudo bom?” They both mean “how are you?” and “everything is good” and they may be both a query and an answer.

Thus, if someone responds “tudo bem?” you react with “tudo bom!” And if someone asks you “tudo bom?”, react with “tudo bem!”

3. Greetings for every time of day

If you wish to greet people appropriately throughout the day in Portugal, there are three essential Portuguese phrases to learn:

Bom dia – Good morning.
This may be only used in the morning before lunchtime.

Bom tarde – Good afternoon.
This phrase is used between noon and 6 pm.

Good night - Boa noite.
At 6 pm onwards, utilize this one. You may also use it as a general method of saying farewell.

Tip: When pronouncing “bom dia”, don’t pronounce “bom” like the English word “bomb”. The -om ending is a nasal vowel, so instead of shutting your lips to utter the “m” sound, you let the air out of your nose and mouth to just speak the “o”. That may be tough so if you’re having problems, pronounce “bom” like the English word “bong”. It’s closer to the right pronunciation than “bomb”.

4. Glad to meet you – Prazer

If you’ve made a new friend on your vacation to Portugal, make sure to give them a courteous “prayer” (good to meet you) (nice to meet you)

5. Farewell – Adeus

If you say hello, you should also learn how to say goodbye. Much as in English, there are many various ways to say farewell, depending on the circumstance. One of the most prevalent terms is “that”. It’s pronounced like the Italian “ciao”.

If you’d want a more formal way to say farewell, you might use “adeus”, which is comparable to the Spanish phrase “adios”.

6. Pardon me – Com licença

There are many distinct applications and methods to say excuse me in Portuguese.

If you're walking through a throng and need to respectfully urge someone to get out of your path, you may say "Com licença" or simply "licença".

If you need to ask someone to repeat what they're saying, you may say "a como?" or "o que disse?" This also translates to "excuse me?"

If you need to apologize for bumping into someone, or you're trying to catch a waiter's attention, you may say "Desculpa" which also means "excuse me".

7. Please – Por favor

If you're searching for some basic Portuguese words that can help you be a bit more courteous and respectful on your vacation to Portugal, don't forget your pleases and thank yous!

You may add "por favor" (please) to the end of a statement to make it more courteous. For example, if you wish to ask for the bill at a restaurant, you may say to the moço (waiter): "Você puede trazer a conta, por favor?" (Can you bring the bill please?)

8. Thank you – Obrigado(a/o)

The method to express "thank you" in Portuguese varies based on your gender. If you're female, say "obrigada". If you're masculine, say "obrigado". You may also abbreviate it to "brigada" or "brigado".

You may also say "de nada" (you're welcome) after some thank you.

9. Yes – Sim

This is one of the most basic Portuguese phrases yet it's a crucial one.
Like the word "bom", sim also has a nasal vowel. If you're having difficulties pronouncing it properly, try speaking it like the English word "sing".

"Yes" in Portuguese is sim. Like bom above, the sim has a nasal vowel. At a first approximation, it sounds like the English word "sing".

10. No – Não

It's one of the most fundamental Portuguese terms to know yet it'll come in useful. No is "não", pronounced similarly to the English "no".

11. Where is… ? – Onde está…?

If you've recently arrived in Portugal, you might need some additional help finding your way about. If you need to ask for directions, say "onde está…?" (where is…?)

These are some simple Portuguese phrases to learn to help you explore Portugal:

Onde está a house de banho? - "Where is the bathroom?"
Onde está an estação de comboio? - "Where is the railway station?"
Onde está a parada de autocarro? - "Where is the bus stop?"

12. What is your name? – Qual é o seu nome?

If you want to get to know someone, ask their name by stating "Qual é o seu nome?"

You may then tell them your name by stating "O meu nome é or Me chamo…" (My name is…).

13. How much does this cost? - Quanto custa isso?

If you're intending to do some shopping in Portugal, one of the greatest basic Portuguese phrases to learn is "Quanto custa isso?" (how much does this cost?).

14. I don't understand – Eu não entendo

If you're new to studying the Portuguese language, you'll likely have some problems comprehending anything at first. Let folks know when you've lost them by saying "Eu não entendo" (I don't understand). You can also say "O quê?" (What/Say that again?)

15. Do you speak English? – Fala inlgês?

If you're truly suffering and need to find someone who can speak English, it's courteous to ask them first instead of presuming they can speak your language. You can say "Fala inlgês?" (Do you speak English?) Alternatively, let them know that you don't speak Portuguese by saying "Não falo português". You may even remark "Eu estou aprendendo Português" (I am studying Portuguese) and others may even aid you with some fundamental words.

Greetings and Popular Phrases

People are the soul of a country. Learning simple Portuguese greetings will go a long way when engaging with native Portuguese speakers. As with every language, Portuguese has numerous distinct methods to welcome people and communicate basic niceties. This article contains the must-know Portuguese terms and phrases for welcoming people. Let's dig right in!

Ways to say "hello" in Portuguese

Olá

"Olá" is the greatest choice and go-to solution for most social occasions regardless of the person you are addressing. Translated to "hello," It's strangely official, but also pleasant. Don't mix this with the Spanish "hola." In Portuguese, the stress lies on the second syllable.

Oi!

"Oi!" is a very warm and informal way to say "hi!" It is more often used in Brazil than in Portugal and is used to welcome friends and close coworkers. Adhere to "olá," though with folks you don't truly know.

Alô

This one is borrowed from English and is especially exclusively used on the phone. It may be utilized while answering the phone or mid-phone conversation if the line begins failing and you're having problems hearing each other.

E aí?

Though the phrase technically translates to "what's up" it is used as a replacement for "hello." This is mostly used in Brazil and amongst the younger generation.

Como é que é?

The Portuguese counterpart of the one above is "como é que é?" which directly translates to "how is it?"

Beleza?
"Beleza" also has a similar connotation as "e aí," yet it translates to "what's going on with your life?" This is generally casual and frequently used to welcome close friends.

Greetings for specific moments of the day

Bom dia
"Bom dia" actually means "good day," but you'd only use it to express "good morning" in Portuguese. Notice that Brazilians pronounce "dia" as "jee-ah" while the Portuguese speak "dee-ah."

Boa tarde
Meaning "good afternoon" in Portuguese, it is used between luncheon and sundown.

Boa noite
The Portuguese language does not discriminate between evening and night. Hence, "good night" and "good evening" have the same translation in Portuguese. Though "boa noite" technically translates to "good night," it is used as a greeting and not something to say to someone before they go to bed, like in English.

"How are you" in Portuguese--Tudo bem/bom?

This one is excellent for both professional and informal occasions. "Bem" means "well" and "bom" means "good," you may choose either which makes this greeting translate to "everything well?"

Tem passado bem?

If the one above is a touch too informal, then "tem passado bem?" is suitable for those formal circumstances. This one directly translates to "have you been passing well?"

Como vai? -Como está?

Translated to "how are you?" this Portuguese greeting is frequently said soon after saying hello.

Saying farewell in Portuguese-Até logo/Até amanhã

Translating to "until later" and "until tomorrow" respectively, these Portuguese expressions are great for informal circumstances or when "goodbye" is a touch too forceful for the occasion.

Tchau!

This one is used in various languages. Similarly, many nations, use the term "that" when saying farewell at the end of a conversation. Note that it may also be spelled as "you!"

Adeus

"Adeus" literally translates to "goodbye," but, be careful with when and how you use this phrase. "Adeus" suggests that you will never truly see the individual again or at least that you don't intend to. Keep this term for sad or tragic goodbyes instead.

With Portuguese being a language that touches the four corners of the earth, it's also crucial to consider regional variances when learning Portuguese greetings.

Portuguese Etiquette

Portuguese Etiquette while welcoming or greeting other persons is paramount to be aware off.

It is a common greeting in a formal environment to shake hands first. You do this generally when you have not met the individual previously or if the folks you are meeting are not family members or close friends.

In most social occasions, the handshaking is done by eye contact and the customary Portuguese pleasantries. The handshake is also done while leaving. Informally, friends and family members embrace or clap one another on the back (men) or kiss both cheeks (women).

Ladies shake hands if they do not know each other or in very casual circumstances. Portuguese people are straightforward in speaking with others; they tend to convey the truth, even if they are courteous.

First names are used to address friends, youth, and family members. Adults should be addressed by their last name or the title paired with their first name. You have to listen attentively and learn what individuals like to be called.

Bear in mind that Portuguese will be formal in public and will enter into a more direct conversation when alone or in particular circumstances when there is greater privacy. So, it is advisable to follow the same pattern and be courteous during official occasions and speak your heart in private moments.

Likewise, remember that Portuguese individuals can speak swiftly and, at times, loudly. That is part of their culture and usual to witness. That doesn't imply they are upset or furious with you.

Conclusion

Going to Portugal is an adventure of a lifetime, and the Portugal Travel Guide is the perfect companion to take you around the nation. From its magnificent beaches to its ancient cities, Portugal is the perfect place for a holiday. With its rich culture, wonderful cuisine, and gorgeous surroundings, Portugal has something for everyone. With this book, you can be sure that you will have the vacation of a lifetime, and you will be able to discover the finest of Portugal. Thus, if you're seeking a terrific holiday spot, then look no further than Portugal. The Portugal Travel Guide will be the perfect companion to help you make the most of your time in the country. So, what are you waiting for? Come to Portugal and enjoy a trip that you won't forget.

With the guidance of a competent guide, tourists may explore the nation to its greatest potential, learn about its history, customs, and culture, and enjoy the time of their lives. A visit to Portugal is an experience that will be remembered for a lifetime and one that should not be missed.

Printed in Great Britain
by Amazon

20207799R00098